About the Author

Having spent his entire life touring and travelling the world, Jim Toomey has finally settled down in Brisbane, Australia where he now lives with his young family.

Still playing occasional gigs in a jazz and blues trio, Jim has recently turned to writing and does some acting work, appearing as an extra in the latest Pirates of the Caribbean movie.

Turning professional in 1965 at the height of the beat boom in England, he survived the hippie revolution and highs and lows of life as a rock musician in a variety of bands. Jim was a founder member and drummer in The Tourists from day one.

To Tomoko Oka

Jim Toomey

WE WERE TOURISTS

AUSTIN MACAULEY PUBLISHERS™

LONDON • CAMBRIDGE • NEW YORK • SHARJAH

A CIP catalogue record for this title is available from the British Library.

ISBN 9781786935526 (Paperback)
ISBN 9781786935533 (Hardback)
ISBN 9781786935540 (E-Book)
www.austinmacauley.com

First Published (2018)
Austin Macauley Publishers Ltd.
25 Canada Square
Canary Wharf
London
E14 5LQ

Acknowledgments

I would like to acknowledge:

The late Peter Coombes – the writer of nearly all the songs we ever played.

Eddie Chinn – one of the nicest people on the planet and bass man through and through.

Dave Stewart – the most eccentric and crazy person I ever met, one of the best guitarists, songwriters and producers in the world.

And of course the amazing Annie Lennox – the singer and writer of beautiful songs, the weaver of dreams, the world peace advocate.

Also, the many friends that helped the band in the early days. David Wernham, Alistair Crawford, Olaf Wyper, Jeff Hannington, Lloyd Beiny, Dave Wright.

Celia Shafron, Nassim Khalifa, Paul Jacobs, Ms Penny Blue, Katherine Wilkins De Francis, Ralph Denyer.Chris Howell.

The production team at my publishing company Austin Macauley. With special thanks to Connor Browne for his belief in my story and help with my incoherent scribbles. Also the staff at XIX Entertainment and Steve Gayler at The Ultimate Eurythmics, Annie Lennox, Dave Stewart Fan Club. Also, Pavel Jary for his help and input. Lastly I would like to acknowledge my wife Tomoko Oka for putting up with me and for her invaluable help and support.

Foreword

By Dave Stewart

I first met up with Jim Toomey when I stumbled into a studio in Tin Pan Alley in London high on Psilocybin Mushrooms mixed with amphetamines and a handful of Moroccan hashish as a calming agent. I'd been up all night and feeling a little worse for wear, but as always I managed somehow to appear relatively straight – or so I thought!

Annie and I were inseparable and had just come from the squat we were living in North London above our mate's record shop (which was also a squat). I already knew that Annie and I were going to do something magical together but this wasn't the time or place, we had to work hard, pay our dues and patiently wait.

Jim was and still is a very "upbeat" positive person, he's been round the block a few times but he was a very professional drummer and later I found out he also knew how to make mushroom tea and hash cookies!

Jim also knew how to use a lighting system and often operated the spotlight for his girlfriend Penny Blue, a legendary London striptease artist, which I found highly impressive.

Annie and I traveling around the world performing as The Tourists probably had a completely different experience to the others (Peet Coombes, Jim Toomey and Eddie Chin) because we were a couple and did everything together. Annie was the only girl and we were often crammed in a van driving overnight, zig-zagging around the USA, Europe and Australia trying to keep sane and stay alive! Our relationship as a couple was put through the most insane tests of endurance yet somehow we got through it, even surviving drunken pilot flights in the Caribbean, plane wings catching fire in Australia, but most of all surviving the crazy journey of being a Tourist.

The music business sucked – it still does – there were and are sharks everywhere, at least back in those days you could see them. Now they are hidden behind giant corporate walls using tiny robots to do their dirty work.

I'm so glad Jim is alive happy and has a family. He's still playing drums in Brisbane, as enthusiastic as ever (you should go watch him). Positivity is the best youth serum for sure and Jim has plenty of it!

What Jim will reveal in this book is a drummer's eyewitness account. Sometimes his view may have been blurred by the cymbals and a few shots of neat alcohol or maybe a knife blade full of cocaine, but he kept whacking those things night after night and I'm grateful for it. I learned so much playing countless gigs with Jim in The Tourists, from tiny clubs to major concert halls; he nailed it every time. Annie and I are thankfully still alive and well. I leave you with this quote:

"That which does not kill us, makes us stronger."
Friedrich Nietzsche

Preface

Andy Warhol once famously said, "In the future, everyone will be world-famous for 15 minutes" Well it was our turn I guess, although Dave Stewart and Annie Lennox seem determined to prove him wrong!

"We Were Tourists" is a classic rags to riches story.

I was lucky enough to be the band's drummer from day one. We were together for 3 years, selling well over 500,000 singles and over 100,000 albums. Yes I have my gold and silver discs on my wall, frozen in time, like Warhol's ducks in flight.

The following story is totally as it happened, or as close to it as I can remember.

The Magic Bus

Dolly Parton's bus was a bit like a motel.

The only difference being of course it moved.

We had TV – Video – Mega sound system – Lounge – Kitchen – Sleeping bunks, and our very own southern gentleman bus driver complete with CB radio and racist attitude. The tour of America had been going forever. Starting in New York we did well in the clubs and pulled off a good recording which was broadcast as a live gig. Reviews were good but we were immediately wrongly described as one of the new English punk bands. The Pretenders and The Police who were also slogging round the clubs at that time suffered the same fate. We went upstate and did well in places like Boston playing mostly to university kids but as we moved further away from the east coast the crowd's attitude seemed to change. The Midwest was not ready for punk bands it seemed. We played some tough places on that tour, but we soldiered on. Annie was amazing and completely took over the stage some nights becoming almost aggressive in her attitude, turning the negative energy back on the crowds.

So now here we were in Texas. The distance between gigs was so great the road crew and band had to travel at night to keep to the schedule. Hence Ms. Parton's bus. We would come off stage and pile into the bus to travel through the night to the next gig, this madness had been going on for a week or so. One particular night it was Peet's birthday and Annie had decorated the bus with balloons and streamers. I think by then we were in Colorado. We pulled away from the gig and travelled and partied through the night. I can remember all of us singing the old pub song 'Show Me the Way to Go Home' and Dave and I speaking to astonished truck drivers on the CB radio. I remember asking in my best drunk English posh voice, "Could I enquire as to the name of your handle?"

Eventually only Peet and I and the cowboy were left. I was extremely drunk when Peet pulled a small bottle from his bag. He warned me it was 100% alcohol and that I couldn't match him shot for shot. Well I tried but I must have passed out. The next thing I remember is waking to an empty bus and being deafened by what sounded like a waterfall. I staggered to the driver's compartment expecting to see Niagara Falls. I was amazed to see a sea of umbrellas and a busy street full of people going to work. It slowly dawned on me it was pouring with rain and we were parked outside a hotel. I was locked in.

My mouth felt like the bottom of a parrot's cage. I pushed all the buttons I could find hoping the doors would swing open. Nothing worked. Then I noticed a tiny side window that was just big enough to put my arm through. I started waving to the umbrellas but nobody stopped. 'Help,' I shouted. 'I'm locked in here.' After a while a friendly black face appeared. A middle-aged lady had seen my frantic waving. She seemed a bit taken aback at the sight of a skinny white face with bright red spikey hair and eyes to match. I pleaded with her to help me and asked her where I was. 'Well, young man, you are in Denver, Colorado and outside The Howard Johnson Hotel.' I asked her if she would be good enough to go to the hotel reception and ask to wake the driver as I was locked in. She smiled and disappeared. After a while the doors hissed open and there was our grumpy Texan still with his hat on. Apparently everyone had tried to wake me to no avail. I gingerly entered the hotel and got my key.

I must have slept till the evening as I was woken by the bedside phone. 'Come on, Jim, it's almost sound check time.' It was Kevin, our American tour manager. I showered and made it to the restaurant and ordered a BLT and coffee.'

'Hi Jim, how are you feeling?' The question came from a pretty young waitress. 'You were so funny at breakfast today.' I had no idea what she was talking about, or who she was. The coffee was delicious and slowly I began to focus. I was getting smiles from the other staff members too. "Hi Jim, how are you? Have a nice day." Two beautiful girls wearing air hostess uniforms walked by. 'See you tonight.' 'Okay see you.' I was beginning to enjoy myself except I couldn't remember why. Then another complete stranger came over and joined me at the table. 'Hi Jim, is your room okay?'

Well that was enough. 'Okay,' I said, "who are you?" 'Well don't you remember? I am the hotel manager. We met this morning when you changed rooms - twice!' I tried to apologise. 'Oh no need, you were very polite and funny, in fact you had everybody in stitches.' Was I? Did I?

Apparently I had walked straight from the bus and into the breakfast room an invited the whole crew of an American Airways flight to the gig that night. I had proceeded to tell jokes and my life story to anyone that would listen. I had then decided that my room was facing east and was too bright and my second room was above the sixth floor and therefore above the level of fire trucks ladders in case I had needed to be rescued!

And so the tour went on, seemingly forever. The Holiday Inns had identical rooms no matter what state you were in. The same carpets, the same furniture arrangements and even the same tacky pictures hanging above the beds. We were all going a bit crazy. I got up for breakfast one morning to be confronted with Dave and Annie who were quite happily roller-skating along the corridors waving to everybody.

How did I get here? What on earth happened?

I Am Not A Tourist –
I Live Here

I should really start at the very beginning, in fact three years earlier.

I had set my drums up in the studio; it was 9 a.m. I went through the usual nightmare of finding a parking space in the notorious part of London's West End known affectionately as Tin Pan Alley.

Logo Records had booked me to record a series of demos for three new songwriters they had just signed. My career was going well. After years of touring with a variety of bands and artists through the late sixties and seventies my reputation as a freelance session drummer was paying off. I spent my days going from one studio to the next and had recorded and toured extensively with Colin Blunstone, Titus Groan, Jet, and Mick Ronson, amongst others. Earning your living from recording studios wasn't as much fun as playing live and most of the singles and albums I played on were pretty uninspiring, my all-time low was recording an album with Rolf Harris.

The bass player booked for the session was Andy Brown, one of the top players in London at the time. Andy is a great guy with a great sense of humour which came in handy with some of the music we sometimes had to record.

It's 1977 and the London music scene had completely gone a full circle. The euphoric days of the swinging sixties and the subsequent hippie revolution are suddenly over. Bands like Cream are finished. The whole concept of Supergroups and Superstars has backfired on a new and younger generation hungry for something new and exciting. In a small sex shop in Kings Road a young and extremely ambitious Malcom McLaren stumbles across a bunch of young deviants. They are unemployed but they have a rock band and perhaps more importantly they have an attitude.

Well Andy and I had an attitude – we were being paid by the hour. We tuned up and were ready to go at 10 a.m. I found out from the studio engineer that one of the songwriters was Dave Stewart. I knew Dave from when he was in a band called Long Dancer. They had signed to a new company called Rocket Records. Unfortunately for Dave Rocket Records had also signed a singer-songwriter called Reggie Dwight who promptly, and wisely, changed his name to Elton John. Long Dancer were left in the shadow of Elton's massive popularity and the band had split.

The first to arrive was Pete Coombes. He seemed pleasant enough but seemed a bit unsteady on his feet. His hair was unkempt and he was wearing a cheap shoddy suit that looked as if he had slept in it. He seemed pleasantly stoned, even at that time in the morning, little did I know at the time, but it was a sign of things to come. He produced two rather battered guitars, one acoustic and one cheap electric which had only five strings.

Things were looking up. I caught a glimpse in Andy's eye as he casually glanced at his watch. The engineer bravely helped Pete string the electric and plug him in and as soon as I had the guitar in my headphones we started to jam over a few riffs. By this time I could see Dave in the control room along with a tall slim girl with a shock of blond hair cut in the modern punk style. They came in and introduced themselves. Dave looked totally different than the last time I had seen him. He had gypsy style long earrings and had grown his hair long and it was dyed vivid red and he was sporting a goatee beard. He looked a bit like a Hippy Texan cowboy with long boots and a country and western style shirt and jacket. Annie was stunning, the complete opposite of her partner. She was neat and tidy and dressed in the latest punk style, tight straight leg trousers and a vivid red top which clashed marvellously with her blond spiky hair.

Dave introduced her, we shook hands. Immediately her striking looks and her broad Scottish accent completely mesmerized me, I remember thinking what an unlikely couple they were. She had been introduced to David by Paul Jacobs, a mutual friend of ours. A wonderful character, a streetwise cockney kid and record store owner. Paul was cool, he was the Fonz.

Paul had spotted Annie in a health food restaurant in fashionable Hampstead where she was waitressing. He had chatted her up and learnt that she had auditioned and been accepted into the prestigious Royal Academy of Music in London. Annie had been living with her parents in Aberdeen before that and she had taken the opportunity to leave Scotland and hit the bright lights of London. She had originally wanted to be a professional classical musician but found the staid atmosphere of the academy stifling and had dropped out. Annie was looking for a band. She had studied piano, harpsichord and flute but amazingly her tutors at the academy had completely overlooked, or more likely ignored, her outstanding and unique vocal abilities.

The story goes that Paul took Dave late one night to the restaurant. Dave was wearing his midnight cowboy outfit and had a bleeding earring which I guess completed his pirate image.

He had somehow managed to impress the young Annie enough to see her again and hear the songs she had written. Dave told me later that from the first time he saw her he had felt an instant attraction that was stronger than anything he had ever experienced.

Within days of that first meeting they started a torrid love affair that was to last for the next three years. They had moved in together to an apartment above Paul's record shop in Muswell Hill.

Time Is Money

Dave set up his guitar and Pete gave Andy a crumpled piece of paper with a rough guide to the chord changes to one of his original songs. Dave started a riff – Andy and I found the downbeat and joined in. Just as I was beginning to think it was going to be another boring session – it happened. Annie's voice suddenly burst into my headphones. She was perfectly in tune and her voice dipped then darted over the chords, bringing the song to life in an instant. I realised at once why Logo Records had signed them.

Her voice soared from a sad lament one moment, to an outrageous crescendo the next, all the while maintaining perfect pitch with an almost aggressive delivery. It was a scary experience to hear a singer with such a range to her voice. A song called 'Why' which she later recorded on her first solo album is a perfect example of this - it says it all for me. It has the most emotional and incredibly complex vocal line; buried deep in that song you will find the real Annie Lennox.

In one hour I think we recorded four backing tracks mostly at breakneck speed. It had been a while since I had broken into a sweat in a studio and I found it exhilarating. Andy too had been blown away by the quality of the songs and we both stayed to listen back to the tracks and of course Annie's vocals.

In the weeks that followed I was asked along with Andy to help form and join the band. As much as I had enjoyed playing on the demos I didn't really want to commit myself to a full time gig and Andy felt the same. Dave insisted we had a meeting with the record company which turned out to be a very bizarre affair. We must have looked an unlikely bunch.

I had learned that Annie had given up her waitressing job and thrown her lot in with Dave and Pete and that all three were on the dole. Dave had been playing some gigs around town with Pete, an old Sunderland mate of his, before that they had been aimlessly busking around Europe dropping lots of acid. This had done little for their health or their songwriting and they had returned to London broke. Annie had been checking the weekly music papers in the musicians wanted columns and had sung in a folk group and even a jazz band to try and find a direction that she felt comfortable with to no avail. Peter Coombes who later changed his name to Peet (and is called so in the rest of this book) was a prolific songwriter. Often tripping on acid and drinking to excess, he would compose words and music at an incredible speed. Dave willingly joined in, often playing guitar and tripping into the small hours with the lovely Annie by his side completely straight and seemingly blissfully unaware of the state of her fellow songwriters.

It was Annie's voice that was to be the icing on the cake. Her ability to complement Peet's melodies and often rambling lyrics by just singing along with him created an unusual unison sound. The downside of this was of course that she rarely got to sing completely on her own and was not singing her own songs or lyrics, this proved to be an ongoing problem to haunt the band on all three albums to come.

Logo Records had a brand new office. It was tastefully decorated and lacked the usual frantic showbiz façade of ringing telephones and dolly secretaries. So there we were. The spaced out Dave Stewart with cowboy boots, weird offbeat clothes and shoulder length red hair. Next to him his partner in crime and fellow Sunderland dropout Peet Coombes, he was wearing his best 'I'm a misunderstood artist' expression and baggy op-shop outfit. Annie Lennox looking prim and proper, bright and chirpy like a virgin ready for the slaughter and Andy and I, the London streetwise pro musicians at that time only interested in making a few quid then on to the next project. Olaf Wyper and Geoff Hannington have a respected background in the music industry working in a variety record companies. They were the proud new owners of Logo Records. They had bought out Transatlantic Records which had an impressive list of recording artists and songwriters including the guitarist Bert Jansch and his band Pentangle as well as John Renbourne. Initially it was, I guess, the folk sound of Peet's songs that had attracted them but they explained they were looking for a major act to establish. To my surprise they had laid out a five year plan for the development of the band as a songwriting team. Their obvious enthusiasm and yet casual attitude rubbed off on all of us. They were asking us to sign a six album deal which would put us under contract till 1984.

The band needed a manager to negotiate a deal but didn't have one. After browsing through the established management companies at the time we eventually signed with David Wernham and later with a company called Arnakata. This proved to be the second major mistake the band had made as Arnakata was recommended by Logo. An advance was paid but both companies took advantage of our mixture of naivety and the frustration of waiting to get it all over with. All we wanted was to get out on the road. I had found out that my fellow band members had walked in off the street and had sat in Logo's office and sang and played guitars. They were immediately offered a worldwide publishing contract with a five hundred pounds advance each. I think they had signed the next day.

Our meeting concluded with Andy and I being put on a wage and not having to sign any contracts. This left us free to freelance with just a verbal agreement to rehearse, record, and eventually play live. And so the big adventure began.

I was living at the time in a large house in Hendon in North London sharing with a bunch of muso's. The owner of the house was a wonderfully eccentric guitar player called Alistair Crawford. Alistair had been the director of a successful paint factory but had become involved with the thriving London underground scene and had completely dropped out of the corporate world. Alistair had become the definitive hippie. His hobbies included growing marijuana and running a recording studio which was basically the large living room of the house. He successfully soundproofed the large front room and had set up a combined rehearsal and recording studio with partitions for a drum booth where we spent many stoned hours getting an acceptable drum sound. He recorded onto two revox tape recorders which in effect gave us four tracks and the ability to overdub and mix. Joan Armatrading recorded some demos there and even The Troggs and somewhat incredulously even Johnny Ray, the American crooner, graced our front room to record. I put it to Jeff Hannington that we could rehearse and record demos there without the usual restrictions of studio time or being charged by the hour. Not surprisingly this was agreed and I found myself in the enviable position of being paid to get out of bed and slide downstairs and get straight on my drums. On the day of the first day of rehearsals I was amazed to find Dave and Annie on the doorstep promptly at 10 a.m. all ready to go.

This was only my second meeting with Annie. Annie was born on Christmas Day and was at that time 21. She was painfully shy at first and made us all tea while Alistair and Dave shared an early morning joint of home grown. I had heard through the grapevine that Dave was a bit of a larrikin. This turned out to be somewhat of an understatement. He has a completely offbeat sense of humour which makes it difficult to know when he is being serious. I was to find out that Dave is very accident prone and freely admits to being a complete hypochondriac. He told us that just prior to meeting Annie he had not one, but three, fairly serious accidents and at that first rehearsal he related the following story.

He had been driving home late one night after a gig with Peet. He had dropped a trip at the gig and had made it all the way back to London and had dropped Peet off.

With just a few blocks to go, just as he started the descent down Muswell Hill, the van's brakes had failed. His face lit up as he described the heady feeling of gathering speed with only the handbrake to slow the van down. On board was the band's gear and an assortment of pills in jars which he had scored earlier that day. Apparently he narrowly missed the clock tower at the bottom of the hill and had shot up the other side on two wheels heading straight for the police station. He had jammed on the hand brake. This resulted in the van flipping onto its side and sliding neatly to rest on the steps of the police station. Dave had rolled out along with his jars of pills and found himself staring at a large pair of boots belonging to a burly sergeant. When the two night duty policemen realised that this red haired crazy person who had rolled to their door along with his drugs and vehicle was not injured, they had made tea. Dave chatted and told stories and when they were out of the station helping the pickup truck he dropped a tab of acid into each cup. This led to lots of laughter between the three of them till dawn. Then Dave had said, "Ah well time to go," and just collected his jars off the table and walked out the door! As unlikely as the story might seem Dave swore on his goatee beard that it was all true and that charges were never laid.

Destiny

Meeting Annie was undoubtedly the best thing ever to happen to him.

In lots of ways Annie is the complete opposite of Dave. She was neat and tidy and more importantly extremely organised. Her disciplined way of life slowly rubbed off on Dave but to me he has never lost that larrikin spirit. In the three years I was to spend with them their relationship survived the almost continuous touring, the ups and downs of everything rock and roll could throw at us, and the recording of three albums. They survived as a couple on the long tours of America and Europe and the transition from being on the dole to major recording artists with silver and gold albums. Annie had an incredible ability of retaining a sense of normality while the rest of us would go out and party after gigs. Dave held it all together though while Eddie, Peet and I would go anywhere and Peet especially would take anything that was on offer. My addiction however was mostly the pursuit of female company which of course didn't go down too well with Annie. Unfortunately I did find myself introducing more than one or two girls to Annie while on tour. To her credit she was always polite and friendly in a professional sort of way but it must have been difficult. Also for Dave it must have been difficult at times to remain faithful in some of the situations we found ourselves in. The extraordinary quality in their later songwriting in Eurythmics and as individual writers must have been bubbling just under the surface for the whole three years we spent together in The Tourists, but Peet just kept churning out those amazing three minute classic songs.

The rehearsals progressed at an amazing pace. One thing that I have always remembered was on that first day, our first rehearsal. I suggested we jam over a funk/rock 12 bar blues. Annie was on keyboards. Dave set it up on guitar and it sounded okay but Annie was not playing. We stopped and she asked if we could write down the music. It was just a twelve bar sequence but the classically trained Annie couldn't play by ear.

After that Peet would work out the chords and just write down the changes for us and give Annie the changes and the lyrics. We would then jam over them trying different tempos and work on the sequence, usually verse/ verse/ chorus/bridge/ verse/ verse/chorus etc. and out. I was thrilled to get back into the vibe of being in a regular band again and we really started to sound more like a group rather than a bunch of songwriters. Annie soon got into the vibe and her vocals continued to amaze me but she was still singing mostly in unison with Peet. One afternoon we were on a tea and spliff break in the kitchen with Alistair leaving Annie in the studio on her own. She was singing quietly and playing the piano. The song was like a slow lament and the chords she was playing were full of emotion and sadness. We sat and listened. The song suddenly soared into a set of magnificent minor chords and Annie's voice flowed over them. It was a chilling and sad and scary song like nothing we had been playing up to that point. Alistair jumped up and announced we had to record it. Annie being unaware that we had been listening seemed rather embarrassed by the fuss we made over the song. At first she was very reticent to record it. "It's just something I wrote and it's a very personal song which would not suit the band." We insisted and she wrote out the chords. The song is called 'One Step Nearer The Edge' and it was an insight of things to come for Annie, who is now recognised, of course, as one of the most talented singer-songwriters in the world. In fact the song does appear on our third and last album which was recorded in George Martin's studio on the island of Montserrat in the Caribbean—a far cry from the cramped studio in a front room in a house in London.

My mate Andy Brown had missed a few rehearsals as he had recording sessions coming in all the time. The pressure began to tell as he was turning down lucrative recording sessions to rehearse with the band, the time had come to decide and he seemed quite relieved when we told him that we had to let him go. I, on the other hand, felt really comfortable within the confines of a band and I couldn't wait to get back on the road.

Rather than go through the time consuming process of advertising in The Melody Maker and having endless auditions I rang another friend of mine Eddie Chin. Eddie was from Singapore and is Chinese Malay. I had met him through his girlfriend who was a dancer for Pan's People, the resident dancers on the TV show Top of the Pops. Eddie is a good solid bass player and an all-round nice guy. I invited him round to the house in

Hendon. We had already auditioned two or three bass players that Andy had recommended but they seemed like just more session players. As soon as Eddie walked into the room with his bass in hand the mood changed. He was wearing tight leather trousers, a cool reggae t-shirt and a big smile. Eddie had long straight black hair down to his waist and sported a goatee beard. We threw everything at him. From Peet's super-fast punk songs to the reggae feel of 'Ain't No Room'. Eddie fitted like a glove.

Eddie's image completed our dysfunctional look. Later the press was to describe us as visually confusing-which I guess we were. I think our image and music seemed to confuse the music press in particular. To my ears we were writing accessible modern music, well-constructed songs in the genre of Fleetwood Mac rather than The Sex Pistols. Within a few weeks we had recorded enough demos to fill two albums with Peet bashing out song after song almost on a whim it seemed. Most of the material slotted right into the punk style of the day, especially the lyrics which seemed to fit perfectly into the whole punk philosophy. 'Save Me From Myself', 'Useless Duration of Time', 'Nothing Means Nothing To Me', 'Blind Among The Flowers', mostly played at breakneck speed.

During my days on the road with The Colin Blunstone Band I had become friends with another English eccentric; a certain David Wernham. Dave was as bright as a pin and when I first met him he was a promotion manager at Boosey & Hawkes, the world famous manufactures of Premier Drums. He had secured deals for Keith Moon, the infamous drummer of The

Who. Keith had a habit of recycling his drum kits into spare parts on a regular basis which kept Dave busy sending brand new Premier drum kits to all parts of the world. I had introduced Dave to Colin Blunstone and the boys in the band and he did some tour managing for us in the UK and in the States. This led to Dave setting me up with a sponsorship deal securing a beautiful new Premier kit which I had to use on TV and tours. Back in the day Colin Blunstone had been the frontman and lead singer of The Zombies. They had enjoyed two massive hits in the sixties with 'Time of the Season' and 'She's Not There'. Rod Argent was the keyboard player, he was later to find success with his band Argent. I had recorded with Colin on his solo albums; his manager was Barry Krost. Barry also managed a young Cat Stevens and his brother Jack was The Colin Blunstone Band's tour manager in America.

Dave Wernham popped in on rehearsals from time to time, staying till late into the night listening to the songs. He eventually offered us a very fair one year contract to manage the band with options on either side to prolong the contract. We signed and Dave immediately set to work. He was managing an outrageous punk band at the time called The Vibrators and was actively trying to secure them a record deal. We had a record contract with Logo and now we had management and at last some gigs in the book. Our first appearance was at a small pub in Islington in north London called the Hope and Anchor. We were to support The Vibrators. A very young group of Irish lads had played there in their band called U2 a few weeks before and the Hope and Anchor was typical of one of the many new punk venues where new bands

31

could be showcased. I was keen to get back to touring. I hadn't played live since the breakup of The Colin Blunstone Band some six months earlier so to celebrate my comeback I treated myself to a short spikey haircut and dyed my hair red.

The pub was packed full of Vibrators fans and we were only allowed to play one 45 minute show. The dressing room was tiny. Annie looked amazing in her op shop gear which included a black mini-skirt embroidered with sequins and black tights. We all sat and stared at each other. Eddie our shiny new bass player looked like a samurai warrior with his long hair scrunched up with what looked like chop sticks to hold it up. He had only just rehearsed each song once or twice and sat staring at his song list. Peet looked pensive wearing a battered old grey baggy suite with his scraggly hair hanging over his face. Dave on the other hand looked like a 16th century crazy person with his goatee beard, vivid red hair and a brilliant red silk jacket. Annie seemed calm enough and peered out at the crowd that was now standing shoulder to shoulder right in front of the stage. The sound check had gone well as we were using The Vibrators' PA and we had spent some time to get the vocals balanced nicely in the stage monitors. Our energetic manager burst into the room with bottles of beer for the band to carry onto the stage. We filed out and had to push our way through the crowd to get on. The sound system was playing at full volume as we plugged in. My beautiful new Premier drum kit was miked and I had tuned it up loud – ripping off the tape and padding that I usually had to use in studios. Suddenly the in-house music was cut abruptly. Silence.

The stage lights went on and all I could see were the front row of faces. We raced into the first song and immediately Annie threw herself across the stage leaping and dancing all over the place. It was as if she was a coiled up spring that had suddenly been released. She seemed to me to be exorcising the years she had spent cooped up in the music academy, peeling off layer by layer, song by song, her strictly conservative Aberdeen upbringing.

It was an extraordinary performance. We crashed and sped through the setlist, giving the audience no time to catch their breath. Through the lights I could see Eddie reading the chord changes from a list he had gaffed to the stage. We finished with 'Save Me From Myself'. Peet's analyst lyrics capturing perfectly the mood of the time, Annie was bathed in sweat glistening in the lights, spitting out the lines of desperation that were to prove only too prophetic of Peet's ultimate downfall. The crowd's reaction was instant and thrilling to experience. They seemed to sense that they had just seen something very special. We ran off and pushed our way back through the crowd. Back in the dressing room we could still hear the calls for more ringing in our ears. We had blown the room apart. Dave Wernham was ecstatic and informed us he had seen at least two journalists out of the five he had invited at the bar. Eddie and I followed suit and retired to the bar. Eddie is a very cool customer and a man of few words. "So what do you think, Eddie?" I asked, shouting over The Vibrators. His reply was spot on, though not exactly what I had expected. "She is a star."

The Booming Tourist Trade

The next week the New Musical Express gave us a glowing review with a photo and a heading of 'The Booming Tourist Trade'. Dave Wernham went to work. We were soon working three or four nights a week; in fact in that first year we gigged almost continually with the only break being a trip to Germany to record. We would play almost anywhere. Some of the gigs were confrontational to put it mildly. Punk audiences wanted action. Gone were the days of sitting back smoking a spliff and listening and respecting the musicians on stage. Now the general idea was to get up and join the band on stage and cause havoc. The term 'pogo dancing' was invented around this time. This entailed mindlessly jumping up and down on the spot then throwing yourself blindly through the crowd. This was later to develop into crowd surfing and mosh pit diving. All this was exciting for the band with the exception of the disgusting trend of spitting. This usually came from the hardcore kids around the front of the band and for some unfathomable reason they saw it as a term of endearment! Some nights I could see globs of spit flying through the air, nicely lit by our stage lights. All of this madness had an extraordinary effect on Annie. Her stage wear became more and more bizarre, often buying clothes from op shops on the road and altering them to great effect. Her hair by now was super short and spikey and peroxide blond. She had learnt how to handle aggressive audiences by turning the energy back onto them – sometimes becoming almost violent herself in her stage presence. On one particular night in the north of England she picked up a broken bottle that had been thrown on stage. She stopped the band in the middle of a song and dared the person who threw it to come up on stage. Nothing happened then she calmly announced that spitting was very uncool and if one more person were to spit she would cancel the show. Now that takes a lot of courage. I quickly counted in the next song and we sped through the rest of the set and left the stage expecting the worst. We stayed in the dressing rooms until our road crew had finished breaking down the gear and we left, luckily all was well. As the nightly drug and alcohol content increased in the band Annie, to her credit, remained sober and straight and would always be first one up for hotel breakfasts which the rest of us would usually miss.

The music press started to take notice and most of our reviews were favourable, even the hardened NME describing our stage show as "infectious fun". The continuous touring had tightened up the band and we were bursting to record. Dave and Annie booked a German producer called Connie Plank. Connie had a reputation in progressive and underground circles and he had had success with early Kraftwerk records. Logo booked us into his studios in Cologne and we started recording in early March 1979. Connie was a lovely man but for some reason he failed to capture the excitement and feel of our live performances. Our first album was released on the 8th of June 1979 and was simply called 'The Tourists'. All our touring paid off and the initial sales were good as we had built up a large fan base. We immediately went on tour supporting Roxy Music, our first experience of 3,000 seated concerts. We were later to find out that we (The Band) were charged one thousand pounds for the privilege, a good example of our money being spent without our knowledge, (a sign of things to come). The reviews of the album also came out that week, also a sign of things to come, and the start of a love/hate relationship with the English music press. The music publication Sounds described it as a 'confusion of musical excursions' which in many ways it was. We released our first single 'Blind Among the Flowers' which sold quite well and eventually reached no 52 in the charts.

Roxy Music are a great band and Mr. Ferry is a great frontman but their audience were kind of middle class and older than the young kids we were used to in clubs and pubs. Plus on quite a few of the gigs we were playing to half empty halls as people were just arriving or at the bars waiting for the main band. Still, by the end of the tour we were getting the crowd in earlier as we were now getting some airplay on the radio stations. Logo Records were keeping a close eye on sales and as soon as they fell we released the second single from the album which was a slow sad song. In fact it was almost a ballad called 'The Loneliest Man In The World'.

Again according to the press we were breaking all the rules with our young punk audience. Dave rang me late one night and asked if I could be at a studio at 9 a.m.

the next morning to put some drum overdubs on the track as he was re-arranging the song and re-mixing it to make it more commercial. The studio was in the Old Kent Road and it was where Ian Dury and the Blockheads had got such a great sound on the classic 'Sex and Drugs and Rock n Roll' track and the 'New Boots And Panties' album. I arrived to find Dave dancing round the studio basking in the freedom of being able to re-mix and re-arrange. This was a turning point for Dave and another step towards being, as he is now, one of the most sought after producers worldwide. He edited out a verse and I put down some percussion and Dave re-mixed the whole track till it leapt out of the speakers.

As soon as we finished the Roxy Music tour we managed to secure a spot on the biggest TV show at the time, Old Grey Whistle Test. We arrived at the BBC at 9 a.m. having just finished a gruelling 27 nights of concerts playing at full volume. To our amazement the TV studio was tiny with a small stage of sorts and instead of an audience of 5,000 we had two rather bored looking cameramen and a sound guy in a room somewhere looking down on us. We had time for three songs. We decided to start with 'Blind Among The Flowers' which starts with almost a drum solo on three floor toms, after that song we went straight into an almost acoustic intro to the next song of Peet's called 'Another English Day' which Annie would announce, finishing with the new single 'The Loneliest Man In The World'. After spending nearly all our allotted time to get the vocals loud enough in the monitors we ran through the three songs. I had dampened my drums down to save spill into the vocal mikes which Annie and Dave plus the sound engineers really appreciated and we brought down the guitar levels till they were just right. By this time we were a fully proficient recording and touring band – a far cry from that first gig at The Hope & Anchor but we were determined to show we could still capture that urgency and excitement and bring it into the homes of hundreds of thousands of TV viewers. A live TV show is probably the most difficult to pull off. The studio was so quiet you could hear a pin drop as the floor manager counted down 5-4-3-2-1.

ACTION. I pounded into the floor toms setting up a triplet with the bass drum. Eddie joined in on bass then Dave and Peet on guitars. It felt good; the vibe was there and as the vocals came in Annie was on perfect pitch with Peet's vocal just a tab under. As the first song ended the empty room rushed in on us. Annie bravely approached the mike and staring straight at the camera simply said 'Another English Day'. It was Peet's big moment and he was sober. He put in a very emotional vocal also staring confidently straight at the camera. The band crashed back in with the lyric 'the wind is blowing a deadly kiss', with Peet's words reflecting the confusion of the time. "I don't know if I should be saying all this, the wind is blowing a deadly kiss". To my mind this pre-empted and was a premonition of the coming AIDS epidemic. As always with Peet's lyrics you never really knew. The last chord and cymbal crash faded; the empty room had been blown away just like The Hope and Anchor all that time ago. We were elated. Peet and I hit the BBC bar, rubbing shoulders with actors from the Doctor Who set in full costume. Annie was bursting with energy and entered the bar looking stunning. The Tourists had arrived at the BBC and we sensed we had broken through in some way. Peet and I went for it and spent all our per diems at the bar. A band called The Selector were there and I tried very hard to chat up their lead singer Pauline Black who I still consider as one of the most talented and beautiful women in the world. I seem to remember our tour manager stealing my car keys and putting me into a cab which I shared with a rather inebriated Doctor Who, but I might have imagined that.

The use of alcohol in rock music is well documented and there have been many victims of course. When Eric Burdon sang in the classic 'House of the Rising Sun' of alcohol "being the ruin of many a poor boy" he wasn't joking. But in his defence and mine there are survivors and I would like to link this into my story with a flashback to The Colin Blunstone Band and a tour of America I did in 1973 or thereabouts.

The American Dream

"Are you in a rock band?" The American accent was thick and his voice seemed much too loud. I was taken by surprise by the question as the plane nosed its way up and through the early morning London fog. I replied that I was and immediately sank down into my seat to try and avoid further contact. "I always thought you guys slept late and only came out at night," he shouted. He tried to shake hands and gave me a beaming smile. I surrendered and gave him a limp hand which he vigorously shook. "Darrell."

I have learnt to my cost not to be too friendly to strangers on long flights. Hours of pointless conversations with travelling salesmen had left deep scars on my usual friendly demeanour. During a lull in the small talk I searched frantically through my travel bag for a means of defence. A magazine? No – too lightweight. A book? No, Darrel looked book-proof. I checked out his suit, the permanent 'have a nice day' smile and most importantly his clashing bright orange tie. No way, I needed a weapon. My fingers fumbled through the murky depths of my travel bag until I found what I needed. The cold touch of the leather case was reassuring. Slowly I eased it onto my lap and saw his expression change at last. I have a lot to thank Akio

Morita for – the mastermind behind the Sony Walkman. I slid on the headphones. A feature of the Walkman that I have always admired is that it enables you not only to cut off from any attempt of conversation but also to annoy your prey with the tinny sound it emits when on full volume. I let him have it. The tape leapt into action with the sound of a very drunk sounding Dutch announcer screaming through our massive PA. "And now Lardies and Gentlemain all the way from England The Colin Blunstine Barnd". The heavily distorted sound of the guitar intro filled my head only to be joined by bass and keyboards and finally my contribution, thundering drums which almost blotted out the others. We raced into the first song playing live at about twice the tempo of the original recording. At once my hangover returned - vivid recollections panned between the headphones. The hotel bar which we had reluctantly left in the early hours. The boyish pranks at Amsterdam Airport.

The prospect of a night's rest before the flight had disappeared with a phone call from Terry the bass player persuading me out for a quick drink at the Marquee Club. I lunged at the off button. The plane had levelled out and the engines were now purring. I willingly drifted off into that surreal world of inflight half sleep.

I awoke to the clatter of the lunch trolley. The plastic wrapping containing the knife and fork put up its usual resistance and, as I tried to tear and eventually bite my way through, I noticed that our crazy tour manager Jackie had somehow managed to change his seat and was now perched on the other side of my new friend Darrel, who was now trapped between us. Jackie didn't

41

look his best. He too had been involved in our adventures in Holland. His complexion looked like a crumpled pound note and his shock of red curly hair looked as if he had suffered an electric shock. It was Jack's job to keep us to the tight schedule of the American tour that we were speeding toward. Fifty-six gigs starting in New York and taking us through the mid-west down through Texas and ending in California with gigs in San Francisco and Los Angeles. We were a five-piece band and had the same members for the last two years. We had recorded two hit singles and two albums and travelled extensively in the UK and Europe. This had resulted in a close camaraderie; Jack had become like another member of the band and had even been given membership to the prestigious points club. Points could be awarded for a variety of things but mostly were awarded to an individual for charming a member of the opposite sex into staying with them overnight in a hotel or similar accommodation. Points could also be awarded for observations of interest on long drives.

A meeting could be called if any claims were in dispute. Terry the bass player insisted for some reason that he had spotted two female cows mounting each other as we sped through the English countryside one sunny afternoon on the way to a gig. The meeting concluded that two points were due as this was an unusual sighting and had been witnessed. Jack had become president and extended the awards to members of the public in unusual situations, even modes of dress fell under the scrutiny of the points club. Our drunken announcer in Holland for example was immediately awarded 5 points.

Anyway, I digress – back to the story...

The Sweet Smell of Success

The Whistle Test was just the break we had needed. It had been well-received and Logo and Arnakata were over the moon. On that impetus we secured an appearance on the infamous Top of the Pops TV show. From memory we were on with a tacky pop duo called Gin Fizz. *Sorry Bucks Fizz!* They were also managed by Arnakata which is how I guess we got on the show. They were all showbiz and sung boring love songs – mindless watery pop. The girl singer tried to strike up a conversation with Annie in the green room. I sat and watched fascinated as the two women singers tried to communicate. They seemed on different planets – which of course they were. We were convinced that we were performing music that was deep and meaningful and Annie was completely focused on being a band member only. The problem was the more popular we became the more she was naturally becoming the focus of attention. She was singing her heart out every night to lyrics that were not written by her. To complicate matters Peet's songs were getting more and more personal to his take on life, as he saw it. In fact some of his songs were becoming completely inaccessible and seemed to make no sense, except I guess to him. However, 'The

Loneliest Man in the World' was one of his best and was easy to understand.

The Top of the Pops Studio was in the same BBC building as the Whistle Test. I had been watching this show since I was at school. Even at the tender age of fifteen I thought Jimmy Saville and Pete Murray looked completely stupid and out of touch.

Mind you, a diet of Cliff Richard, Sandy Shaw, Val Doonican and Des O'Connor did little to wet my appetite for a career in music until an appearance by The Rolling Stones. My parents immediately hated them. My father dismissed them as rubbish and that was it as far as he was concerned. When I was old enough I started to hang out in the West End of London which was buzzing with live music venues. On leaving school my father had secured me an office job in Leicester Square which is virtually in Soho and close to all the jazz clubs and music shops. I would spend my lunch times wandering through the narrow streets peering at the strip clubs and the posters of bands with names like The Kenny Ball Jazzmen, Chris Barber's New Orleans Feet Warmers and Acker Bilk's Paramount Jazz Band. All these groups played Dixieland/Traditional rather than modern jazz. The music press of the time labelled it trad-jazz and Acker Bilk the jolly clarinet player from Cornwall had a massive hit with a song called 'Stranger On the Shore' which was the first break through to the pop charts. I started to buy a weekly publication called Jazz News which I would proudly display on my commuter daily train trips. I read that Chris Barber and Ken Colyer were the only two groups that played real jazz while the rest just did Trad. Lonnie Donegan was the original banjo player with The Ken Colyer Band before leaving to go commercial. He too had a hit record called 'Does Your Chewing Gum Lose Its Flavour (On the Bedpost Overnight?)'.

Well that was enough for me—at the tender age of 17 I decided to become a New Orleans jazz purist and devote my life to the cause. I had no idea what the cause might be, but I had seen the light! I discovered Dobells Jazz record shop on Charing Cross Road and started buying albums by Bunk Johnson—George Lewis and Jelly Roll Morton. The drumming was very basic—4-4 bass drum and simple snare rolls with occasional tom tom or wood block fills.

My dad used to be a drummer in a dance band playing waltzes and foxtrots. I told him of my interest in drums and he advised me to buy a rubber practice pad and a pair of sticks and play along to the records—so I did. Every night, straight from work, two three or four hours a night. I must have driven my parents mad. One day in town I picked up a music publication called the Melody Maker. This covered both jazz and pop and had features on rock and roll and a thing called R&B. I remember reading a letter from a guitar player complaining that blues music and his band that played rhythm and blues were being ignored by Trad Jazz fans. He went on to say that his band were having trouble getting work because they refused to jump on the commercial bandwagon. A kindred spirit I thought, but what was rhythm and blues? The writer was Brian Jones.

As I had to commute by train weekdays to Charing Cross station I bought monthly train passes and this enabled me to travel to town for free at weekends. An

46

old school mate and I would go to the West End every Saturday and Sunday looking for girls and adventure. We would wonder into coffee shops as at 16 we were too young to go into pubs and clubs. One of these featured live folk music and it was tucked away down a narrow side street off Wardour Street. Mostly the singers were just buskers I guess but one night a scruffy beatnik got up on stage with his acoustic guitar. The first thing that struck me was his hair. It was extremely long and spikey almost down to his shoulders and cut in layers. He wore tight straight leg tartan trousers and chucker boots and a duffel coat. He played some old gospel spirituals and blues standards in total contrast to the other white style country/folk singers on before him. His voice sounded old and bluesy and I was mesmerized by his attitude and appearance. It was in fact a young Rod Stewart just before he was discovered by Long John Baldry. He later joined Baldry's band called The Steam Packet along with Julie Driscoll also on vocals and Brian Auger on keyboards.

The Crossroads/
Stairway to Heaven

One memorable Saturday night my school mate and I were wandering along Charing Cross Road on our weekly pilgrimage to Soho when I heard the unmistakable sound of New Orleans jazz. It was coming from a side street called Great Newport and the music seemed to be coming up from under the road. Then I saw a dimly lit sign that said 51 Club and a stairway leading down to a cellar. I nervously asked the bouncer on the door who was playing. He told us we were in luck as it was the Governor, he ushered us in and charged us 10 shillings each which about a fifth of my weekly wages. As we descended the steep staircase my heart was beating. The heat and sound hit me at once. It was a packed cellar-like room, dimly lit with the band at one end and alcoves where couples were kissing and moving slowly to the beat. The audience was so squashed together there was no room to move let alone dance. I seem to have entered into a fantasy world; sexy young girls were everywhere wearing super tight sweaters and jeans in the beatnik style. The music flowed over me, it was exactly the jazz I had been practicing drums to, but this was real, this was live. I started easing my way towards the stage, it was hot and steamy and exciting and sexy. I had completely forgotten about my friend and somehow lost him in the crowd.

Lost in the moment I decided that there was more to life than the daily routine of office work. I suddenly wanted out, I wanted adventure, but most of all I longed to be on that stage.

I squeezed my way to the front and there they were. The purveyors of this feeling. They seemed like gods moving and weaving to the beat and playing the most emotional music I had ever heard. I was watching the famous Ken Colyer – the trumpet player they called the Governor.

I focused on the drummer. He was soaked in sweat and seemed to be oblivious to the crowd, lost in his drums and cymbals. He was playing just the way I had been practicing, in fact a few of the numbers they did I knew by heart from my record collection. I just stood there drinking in the emotion. I had found my nirvana, I had left the skinny 16 year old virgin at the door and in my mind I was a jazz man. I would play drums on stages all over the world surrounded by girls in tight sweaters and blue jeans. Suddenly it was over. The crowd stayed and watched the musicians file off stage and disappear.

The crowd started to slowly make its way back to the exit. I shuffled along feeling very conscious of the blonde girl next to me. I was clutching my jacket in my hand when I felt the softness of the girl's right breast lightly brushing against my arm. The crowd stopped moving and I nervously glanced at her. She didn't move away – I was in heaven. I felt as if I was paralysed. Her breast was now resting on my hand which was clutching my jacket. She was beautiful and chatting quite happily to her boyfriend seemingly totally unaware of the extreme pleasure her nearness was giving me. We all moved towards the bottom of the stairs and I was pushed away for a second then, there it was again. Harder this time and I swear she glanced at me and smiled, the softness flowed over me, I was praying that we could stay without moving forever. Then in an instant we were on the stairs and into the cold night air and she was gone.

"Jim, what happened to you?" It was my friend. I felt light headed, transported to another world. As we made our way back to Charing Cross station I tried to explain why I felt so elated. Amazingly he had not enjoyed the club or the music and was completely oblivious to the change in me.

The Top of the Pops

So here I was some ten years later living out my dream
and appearing on TOTP – the top TV music show in the
UK. The green room was filling with stars. We shared
with The Police and I renewed my friendship with Stuart
Copeland and Andy Summers. I had played on some
sessions with Andy and I knew Stuart through the
grapevine of contacts leading back to Curved Air, a band
he had played with some years before. I rescued Annie
from Bucks Fizz and introduced her. Although she had
matured enormously and was no longer the shy girl from
Aberdeen it had all happened so quickly that she still had
that innate shyness about her that was, and still is, so
attractive. Dave on the other hand was everywhere,
smiling and chatting. The group Madness came in. Like
us they were making their first appearance and seemed a
bit overwhelmed. TOTP was an easy gig compared to
The Whistle Test, you didn't have to play live but just
mime to your own record. I was given some plastic
cymbals to use. These were made to look exactly like the
real thing and rubber pads had been placed over each
drum. We were announced and our backing track burst
from the monitor speakers. We immediately went into
our animated stage movements—desperately posing as
the live cameras swung and swerved between us.

Miming to music that you have recorded gives you a feeling that you are cheating, which of course you are. The live invited audience know you are, but are of course thrilled to be seen as if the music were live – Andy Warhol was right – everyone is a pop star!

The single had reached number 32 in the charts. We were turning into stars but there was an uneasy feeling in the band, almost as if success was definitely not cool. Well it was cool for me, I was determined to enjoy the fruits of whatever level of fame we might reach. I had managed to renew my relationship with the lovely Penny Blue. Penny was half Jamaican and half English and was a professional stripper, or as the press would put it 'an exotic dancer'. At the age of fourteen she was abandoned and became pregnant. Her son Paul who I was to meet at age 21, was taken from her. I had fallen in love with Penny and I was turning up at her apartment at all hours after gigs. Any nights off we would be hit the clubs and party. Penny was outrageous and I loved her for it and slowly Annie started to relax in Penny's company, but they really could have not been more different. To her credit Annie didn't smoke or drink and certainly did no drugs. In the three years we were to spend on the road I never saw her out of it on anything. Her highs were performing and her relationship with Dave and she seemed completely unaware of the nightly excesses of alcohol and drugs of the rest of the band.

Rose the Gypsie

I remember one day when the most extraordinary thing happened.

We had arrived early enough for some free time in Brighton which is on the coast in the south of England. The gig wasn't till 8 p.m. There is something about Brighton; there is no sandy beach, just piles of giant stones which are splattered with oil from passing tankers. All along the main beach road majestic hotels built in the '30s dominate the skyline. They are painted in bright colours in an attempt to cheer up the visitor and cover up the often grey cold and wet summers. The famous battles of the sixties took place here. Not in 1066, as you might think, but 1966. The fights between the mods and rockers – the teen revolution if you like. The Who's fictitious deaf dumb and blind kid was born here to play the slot machines from Brighton to Soho. Brighton is special, it's like nowhere else. We all wandered off along the pier and Peet, Eddie, Dave and I shared a strong joint of hash. We came across a tent with a vivid red sign. 'Let Gypsie Rose tell your fortune'. Dave and I thought it a great idea. Dave went first and came out after a few minutes, then we all took turns. When I entered the tent it was dark and a bit foreboding. Rose was extremely old and dressed predictably in a colourful dress and headscarf. Her eyes were surprisingly bright and deep blue in sharp contrast to her skin which was darkened by a deep suntan. The deep lines in her face reflecting a long hard life. Her voice was shrill and high pitched, she asked me to cross her palm with silver and stare into the large glass bowl. I felt uneasy as I awkwardly searched my pockets for silver coins. "A crisp pound note will do the trick if silver can't be found." Her voice had suddenly changed and was now deep and low. I placed a note into her hand and she grabbed mine staring into my palm. "There is one among you, but it's not you," she growled. I suddenly felt very stoned as the hash swirled round in my head. She informed me I would be successful and travel the world and leave this island for good and never return.

This was surprisingly accurate as it turned out. The tent felt cold and damp and I wanted to leave. What she said was confusing and didn't make sense to me. I thanked her and quickly left the tent feeling relieved to be out in the fresh air again. Annie didn't want to go in. She was last and would only go in with Dave. I asked Peet and Eddie if they had felt anything strange in the tent but before they had a chance to answer there was a shout. A broad Scottish shrill voice rang out. 'LEAVE THIS TENT!' Dave came flying out his face white with shock, leaving Annie to her fate. Apparently Rose had told him to leave as he was not the one, but Annie was. We waited for what seemed an eternity. Eventually Annie emerged. She seemed to be calm but looked even more pale than usual.

She didn't go into detail but related that the Gypsie told her she was to going to be extremely powerful and become involved in the world's struggles, she would find success and have a very fulfilled life. To this day I still wonder what else Gypsie Rose foretold for Annie, but Rose's prediction for me was totally correct.

Reality Effect

Even though we were gigging five nights a week in clubs all over the UK Peet still found time to churn out lots of four minute songs often with nonsensical complicated lyrics like "when the madness has faded", "Circular Fever" and "in my mind there's sorrow" mixed in with the perfectly simple pop sentiments of songs like "So Good to Be Back Home Again". The problem was Peet was such a prolific writer it left no space for songs from Dave and Annie and in the inevitable interviews with the music press poor Annie was left with the dubious task of explaining the meaning of the songs. Peet point blank refused to do interviews and slowly started to withdraw from the rest of us, often tripping and drinking to excess. To try and capture the excitement of our live performances and get a more commercial sound we hired Tom Allom to produce the second album. He attended rehearsals and managed to weed out the most commercial tracks for us to record and managed to book us in to the famous Olympic Studios in London. My drums were set up in the hallowed drum booth where Charlie Watts from the Stones achieved his classic drum sounds. As usual we recorded at breakneck speed but this time attained a fuller sound than our first album. I arrived one morning at ten to find Annie on her own pounding away on the piano and singing a very catchy melody which I recognised but couldn't place. Tom Allum arrived and immediately started recording a rough demo of the song. There were lots of la la la's as Annie didn't know the words or the correct chord sequence. "I know that song but how does the bridge go," shouted Dave through the headphones. We sent out for the sheet music at once. It was a song written by Hawker and Raymonde called 'I Only Want to Be with You'. An English singer called Dusty Springfield had covered it in the '60s so I decided to give it a '60s-type drum feel. We rehearsed it a few times and it fitted like a glove to the other songs we had already recorded, but it needed something to lift it, to make it more modern. My trusty drum roadie had the answer, he came into the drum booth pointing a knife at me! Instead of stabbing me, as I first thought, he said, "Here, Jim, try this." Perched neatly on the point of the knife sat a small heap of cocaine glittering like frosty snow in the dim studio lights. Wack – two sniffs and away we went. I waited for the red light, counted the tempo out on the hi-hat cymbals at twice the speed we had rehearsed it, and the song came to life. I think we did three or four more takes after that but that first track at a faster speed was chosen and stood out as an obvious single.

I was experimenting at the time with some very early electronic drums. I had a set of Syn drums which were basically two rubber pads on a stand that would react to stick beats and you could vary the sound and pitch. I had been using them on freelance disco sessions and used the dowu dowu sound which was very popular at the time.

To make the drum track sound more modern I distorted the sound coming from the pads and overdubbed it onto the intro with amazing results. Dave said it sounded like a wet fish being slapped against a wall and insisted it be mentioned on the album credits. 'I Only Want to Be with You' was released as the first single off the album and went silver then gold and went on to sell in excess of 500,000 copies worldwide.

But there was a hefty price to pay! 'I Only Want to Be with You' was the first and only cover version the band had ever played, let alone recorded, and what we didn't fully realise at the time, was the first song that featured just Annie singing lead vocals on her own. This pushed The Tourists, as a band, spiralling out of control.

We now had a completely new audience; we had lost the faithful record buyers that appreciated the whole new age, or punk if you like, movement that was happening. They had seen us in a pub or at their university and a lot of them had bought our albums. The new record buyers we were now appealing to were happy to go along with whatever was in the charts that week. Yes they would buy the single and then wait for the next trend to come along.

Arnakata jumped at the chance and jumped onto the bandwagon. They financed new clothes and overnight we had a new look. They also treated us to a special recording to make a video. The theme was retro and we all went along with it as it did suit the song. The video was distributed worldwide to critical acclaim.

Jim's first experiences of jazz played live in the Ken Colyer Club in London's West End.

Geoff Gilbert New Orleans Band featuring Jim (right). The band were all arrested for playing on the plinth in Trafalgar Square during an illegal march for the Campaign For Nuclear Disarmament in 1963.

The Tourists have arrived!!!

Where:

When:

RSVP: (213) 556-4870

Promotional postcard.

Tourists

Tourists

Tourists

THE TOURISTS

THE

ROCK & POP
COLLECTION

83

THE
ROCK & POP
COLLECTION

82

THE TOURISTS

Guitarists Dave Stewart and Pete Coombes were the founder members of this band in 1977, but they soon added Annie Lennox (vocals), Jim Toomey (drums) and Singapore-born Eddie Chin (bass). Spent most of 1978 gigging around and sorting out management and recording contracts, and scored their first major success with the old Dusty Springfield song, *I Only Want To Be With You*, which earned them their first gold disc in 1980.

THE TOURISTS

Formed in 1977 by two guitarists, Dave Stewart and Pete Coombes, who soon added Annie Lennox (vocals), Jim Toomey (drums) and Eddie Chin (bass). They were at a loss for a name until riding on a London bus one day, they spotted the London *Tourist* Information Centre! Began gigging in 1978, and won their first gold disc in 1980 with the old Dusty Springfield number, *I Only Want To Be With You*, their third single.

FIGURINE PANINI
© PRINTED IN ITALY BY EDIZIONI PANINI S.p.A. · MODENA

FIGURINE PANINI
© PRINTED IN ITALY BY EDIZIONI PANINI S.p.A. · MODENA

Tourists Panini stickers.

The Tourists live in Melbourne.

It's The Tourists' season, with a capital T. The Tourists are a four-man, one-woman, London-based outfit who hail from all corners of Britain and points east . . . as far east as Singapore.

The Tourists are:

Ann Lennox . . . . Lead vocals, organ, piano, harpsichord, string synthesizer

Peet Coombes . . . . Lead vocals, electric 6-string and 12-string guitars

Dave Stewart . . . . Electric guitars, acoustic guitar and vocals

Eddie Chin . . . . Bass guitar

Jim "Do It" Toomey . . Drums, percussion, Bolero Dancing and Wet Fish.

Their sound is very much influenced by the eclecticism of the sixties, with a predominant feel of vintage Byrds to the guitar work and melodic structures. If you want to throw in references to the Box Tops, the Groovies and, what-the-hell, the Searchers too, then you'll get a general feel of The Tourists' heavy emphasis on immediate melodic attack and treble dominated guitar drives. —Melody Maker

. . . The Tourists have synthesized their many influences and filtered them through the new wave upheaval to arrive at a blend that is fresh and viable, never just a pointless rehash of past styles. —Trouser Press

Their songs are bright, catchy, very varied and everyone attributed to exquisite good taste. —Musical Express

. . . a fascinating, jangling blend of folk and rock; definitely a Band to Watch. —New York Rocker

Notice that The Tourists are not categorized in any of the above quotations. Their music cannot be labeled. The Tourists are a paint box of influences and personalities, too difficult to assess after one sitting—but leaving a thirst for more and more and more.

Reality Effect has certainly made tremendous inroads in the British music scene. The Tourists' single, *I Only Want To Be With You* is already gold in England where it's already climbed to #4 chart position. *Blind Among The Flowers,* (which was previously released in England off their first Lp and exhibited tremendous success) is a sure fire rocker and is another prime example of The Tourists' versatility. The Tourists are determined to remain eclectic without relegating themselves to any particular cult.

The Tourists will seduce your feet and heart instantly; they're everything pop music should be—irresistible fun, stylish, intelligent and unapologetic.

Give a welcome to THE TOURISTS.   JE 36386

Tourists promotional leaflet.

The Tourists on tour in America.

Jim trying to keep up morale in -20°C at an airport in Sweden.

Paul 'The Fonz' Jacobs.

Jim in the jungle after Annie had stormed off.

(L-R) Dave, Jim (in drag!), Annie at my leaving party, Dingwalls, Camden.

Jim after smashing the windscreen of his 1964 Ford Fairlane 500, bought for a grand from Paul 'The Fonz' Jacobs, who claimed it 'fell off the back of a lorry'.

Jim's wife, Tomoko, with Annie

*Jim with Dave Stewart, Eurythmics' Revenge Tour 1987
(photo by Tomoko Oka)*

Jim pictured recently (photo by Annie Noon, Fotoforce)

The Sweet Smell of Success

Well that did it — everything changed. We had to be everywhere all at once. We were hot, in demand. The single was played to death on high rotation on the BBC and the pirate stations. We were booked again on the TV show Top of the Pops and a embarked on a nonstop 29 date-tour of 5000 seater concerts from Scotland to the south coast of England most of which sold out. The tour went without a hitch with the exception of Manchester.

I've noticed over the years that most musicians and road crew and tour managers on any long tour go a bit crazy after a while. It shows in small ways, from re-arranging hotel rooms in a desperate attempt to make one differ from the night before, to rather more outrageous attempts to be anti-social.

In Manchester Peet and Eddie decided to bomb the hotel. Well not really bomb it in the conventional way, but with stink bombs. They had found a small joke shop in a backstreet near the hotel and bought some stink bombs. These consisted of a selection of small glass vials that when broken would let out the most horrible stink that in a confined space would be unbearable. They spent the afternoon sending lifts up and down with a few glass vials carefully wedged in the well of the sliding doors. When the unsuspecting hotel guests selected their floor number the doors would slide closed and they would not notice the quiet crunch as the glass emitted its horrible load. Eddie and Peet were in hysterics when we got in the car for the short drive to the gig. They thought they had got away with it but just as we pulled away the hotel security man raced out and shouted, "I know who you are."

Just as we were finishing our sound check in the massive Manchester Apollo concert hall I noticed some men arrive wearing suits wandering around looking a bit awkward and completely out of place. I found Dave in the dressing room lighting a massive joint for his nightly hit before the concert. Peet, Eddie and Annie joined us and I mentioned that I saw some strange suits that looked like detectives. We laughed it off and the joint went round as usual. Then it happened, the door flew open and in burst five or six detectives flashing their police badges. "We have reason to believe…" The joint had just found its way back to Dave and I saw him make a fist and dog it in his hand. Everything seemed like slow motion as they searched our stage clothes and bags for drugs. Amazingly they missed the two obvious roaches in the ashtrays and the obvious smell of hash smoke in the air. Eddie and Peet were then warned that anything they say might be used in evidence against them and they were frog marched out of the room and off to the station to be charged.

Well that left Annie, Dave and I staring at the door as it slammed shut. Dave winced as he slowly opened his hand to reveal the remains of the flattened joint and a large burn mark on his palm. Amazingly enough nothing had been found on our five road crew and tour manager so we were okay to play but with only vocals, drums and guitar. Our tour manager immediately got on to a music business lawyer in London and the record company's lawyer and our management's lawyers, all of whom apparently rang the station where the boys were being held. With one hour to go before show time there was still no news. We sat nervously in the dressing room listening to the five thousand or so fans slowly making their way to their seats. At half an hour before the start time we got the call they were on their way. Apparently after being told they would be responsible for a riot of 5,000 teenagers rampaging through the streets of Manchester the police released the jokers and drove them at speed straight to the stage door.

We went on and played a stormer with Annie tapping into the pressure of the last few hours throwing herself around the stage like a swirling dervish. As all the lead vocals were shared with Peet the audience focus would be on both but after a few songs Annie's sheer stage presence would show through and she would become the centre of attention. Annie naturally also took on all stage announcements, a task that Peet, although he had written all the words to the songs, could never achieve.

The tour was selling out everywhere; it was a busy time for us.

SEPTEMBER

18 Thursday Locarno Sunderland

19 Friday City Hall Newcastle

20 Saturday Apollo Glasgow

21 Sunday Capitol Aberdeen

22 Monday Odeon Edinburgh

23 Tuesday City Hall Sheffield

24 Wednesday Town Hall Derby

26 Friday Guildhall Portsmouth

27 Saturday Rainbow London

28 Sunday Odeon Hammersmith

30 Tuesday Gaumont Southampton

OCTOBER

1 Wednesday Colston Hall Bristol

2 Thursday Cornish Rivera St Austell

3 Friday Odeon Birmingham

4 Saturday Odeon Birmingham

5 Sunday St George's Bradford

6 Monday Apollo Manchester

7 Tuesday De Montfort Hall Leicester

8 Wednesday Spa Royal Bridlington

9 Thursday Victoria Hall Stoke

10 Friday Empire Liverpool

11 Saturday Hexagon Reading

12 Sunday Arts Centre Poole

13 Monday University Cardiff

14 Tuesday University Exeter

17 Friday University Leeds

18 Saturday UEA Norwich

20 Monday Stadium Dublin

21 Tuesday Ulster Hall Belfast

The Scam

Our management company suddenly had an extraordinary amount of money coming in. Twenty-seven sell out concerts of an average of 4000 tickets sold at each venue is a great deal of money, plus record sales of 70,000 albums sold and 500,000 singles. Immediately after the tour finished we were called into the office. I remember we had to be there at 9 a.m. We were exhausted but on a high and of course elated with our success.

Two short years after being on the dole we were all seemingly very rich indeed and our beloved management company came up with a plan to send all our hard earned cash off shore to avoid paying hefty taxes. What happened next was like out of a gangster movie.

We were ushered into a room. There was a long table where five serious looking businessmen sat. They all seemed to be wearing matching suits and ties. They had set up a company on the island of Jersey which was apparently at that time exempt from the English tax system. They wanted us to sign contracts that would freeze our assets for two years after which time we would have access. It was a scary moment. We were all given pages and pages of small print to plough through. I looked round the table at the business suits, the tense expressions and the dreadful shirts and ties. Dave seemed amused and flitted through the pages as if he understood every word. Eddie and Dave, the stink bomb kids, stared into the distance and even Annie for once had lost her prim and together demeanour. Lloyd Beanie recommended we have the contracts looked over and recommended a law firm that he assured us were music business experts.

We were of course being set up—the perfect scam. Who in their right mind would trust a firm of lawyers that were recommended by the company that you were in negotiation with? Well we were definitely not in the right mind and certainly in no condition to take on the corporate business world.

After the break-up of The Tourists, Dave told me he immediately gave up all drugs and did a business course and set up a company. The result being D&A, the company he and Annie set up between them. This gave them complete control of their songs including production, publishing and things like merchandising which The Tourists had no control over whatsoever.

Dazed & Confused

We left the meeting with Dave clutching the proposed contracts. The next day the trusty music business lawyers told us it made sense to put all our hard earned cash into their hands and within a week the agreements were signed. Well that was another fine mess we had gotten ourselves into. Be warned all you young musicians, never trust men in matching suits and ties!

Our second Album for Logo had gone silver selling over 60,000 and the single had sold over 500,000, but success is a strange animal, we wanted more. Annie and Dave decided that Logo Records weren't big enough and asked Arnakata to approach RCA to see if we could change labels and break the contracts. I personally liked Olaf Wyper and Jeff Hannington. I was of the opinion that they had done a good job and didn't deserve to lose us to RCA. Arnakarta saw it differently and Lloyd Beiney and Mike Dolan offered to buy the band (probably with our money) from Logo so they could sign us to RCA. Logo refused and a long legal battle started including a court injunction. Logo then took Arnakata to court and lost the first round. Logo then took the case to the high court and Arnakata very kindly lashed out a fortune on lawyers' fees with our money from Jersey - and lost. Bang! We now owed Arnakata around forty thousand pounds. After more pointless negotiations including Arnakata threatening Logo that the band would break up if we couldn't sign with RCA, Logo finally gave up and Arnakata signed us to RCA. That put RCA owning all recording rights. They had bought everything except American royalties. The band was being pulled apart by the very people we had signed contracts with. Still on a high from our success in the UK we were convinced that RCA, being a major company would guarantee our breaking into the American market.

The Big Apple

We set out on low budget tour starting on the East Coast
with endless gigs across Middle America down through
Texas and finishing on the West Coast. We were
following The Pretenders playing the same shows, small
clubs mostly all one night stands. America was a
completely different scene to Europe. Whereas Europe
was buzzing with a new energy involving social change,
a new wave order and punk music, America was
surprisingly conservative. On some nights we would
finish the gig, jump on the bus and travel through the
night to the next one. It was exhausting. We played forty
shows with hardly any nights off. Instead of sleeping
Dave and I would get on the CB radio and marvel at the
accents and language of the truck drivers all of whom
seemed to have radio communication. Our bus driver
was a real Texan cowboy complete with cowboy hat. He
made it very clear that he was anti-drugs but was
continually out of it on Dexedrine which he took to keep
awake and alert during the long night drives. All over
America the press described us as a loud, fast, punk band.
I found Texas to be violent, silently violent. The bus
pulled into a truck stop late one night just near Dallas.
As we walked in you could feel the violence in the air. It

was just like a movie, even the country music coming from the jukebox stopped.

Everyone stared and didn't say a word, just stared. I noticed to my relief two policemen were sitting near the door but they didn't look friendly. We quickly got in line and picked up our trays to choose our hash browns and eggs over easy and bacon burgers. I felt sorry for Annie. She is vegetarian and would spend ages trying to eke out something that she could eat from American set menus which is not easy on the road. As we slid our trays along to the checkout I was amazed to see a selection of knives and hand guns all neatly displayed between the coke bottles and have a nice day cards. Further along there was a cabinet displaying rifles and even a sub-machine gun that I assume you could add to your tray and purchase. We decided on takeaway and fled. The two policemen who were extremely overweight looked on in amazement as if we were from another planet, and of course we were. We scurried past them clutching our takeaways and returned to our moving hotel. At some point in all this madness a message came through from dear old England. We had been booked into recording studios to record our third album as soon as the U.S. tour was completed. That was the bad news, no break. The good news was the studio was located on the island of Montserrat in the Caribbean. This improved morale and gave us hope that we could relax into our third album. The tour wound its way to the west coast where things improved. In San Francisco the audiences were more tuned in to what was happening in modern music and at last we got some good reviews. After a few gigs there we went down to LA and played some of our best received concerts.

The best accolade any musician or band can receive, which transcends record sales or popularity, is when you can attract fellow musicians that you respect to your gigs. Stuart Copeland told me that the biggest personal buzz for him was when The Police played New York in a small club. It was on one of their first U.S. tours. They had recorded a song called 'Roxanne'. Now if you check out the timing on that record there are some amazing time changes between bass, guitar and drums. This resulted in some of the top jazz names turning up backstage to check the band out. Well in our small way we had achieved that in the UK becoming friends with groups like The Specials, The Selector, The Pretenders and even the infamous Lemmy from Motorhead had turned up backstage at our gigs.

We were therefore thrilled when some local L.A. bands turned out to meet us. The Cars turned up backstage one night and I remember Annie being rather overwhelmed at meeting their lead singer Ric Ocasek. The band Blondie was another. Clem Burk their drummer was very excited when he found out I was a Premier Drums fanatic. He was obsessed with English drums and was a total Who fan. We ended up at the Whiskey-a-Go-Go with their entire band except Debbie Harry and our entire band except Annie. They all wanted to meet Annie and of course we all wanted to meet Debbie. Clem asked if I had ever seen The Who live which I had in Switzerland. At that time I was playing in The Colin Blunstone Band and we were booked on the same concert as The Who, so I related the following story.

The Light Side of the Moon

The concert was a major outdoor event just outside Geneva. On the bill was The Small Faces with Steve Marriot, the wonderfully camp Gary Glitter and his band and Argent who were enjoying a big hit with a song called 'Hold Your Head Up'. Top of the bill was The Who. The Swiss promoter had made the mistake of putting all the bands and all the road crews on the same flight out of London. This had led to much camaraderie at the VIP Bar at Heathrow Airport. Bands that are continually on the road rarely get a chance to meet each other to compare notes. All the bands had thoughtfully been seated at the rear of the plane with the notable exception of The Who. They were in Business class which had upset their drummer Keith Moon. He had wanted to party with us at the back. To offset this error in diplomacy as soon as the seatbelt signs were turned off a rather nervous air hostess delivered to each of us a bottle of French champagne with a tag round each neck with instructions from Mr Moon. To be consumed on flight. Soon the corks were popping. Sometime later another air hostess looking even more nervous than the first delivered small parcels to us again with the complements of Mr Moon. Inside mine I found some beautiful G-string black lace ladies undies lovingly wrapped round a vibrator complete with batteries. Also a paper party hat and a packet of edible fruit flavoured ribbed condoms.

Any collection of highly paid and successful people in any profession would, I guess, discuss investments and the world property market. This is not the case with musicians. Successful or not they are normally avid story tellers drawing on the rich vein of continuous travel and a bizarre work environment. This they turn into music and lyrics, from the disposable pop of Gary Glitter to the depth of songs like 'Tommy' or 'My Generation' from The Who.

Well, The Colin Blunstone Band hardly fitted into any of these categories. We were first band on but here we were drinking French champagne, wearing silly hats, and speeding towards a concert playing to thousands.

It was almost dusk when we touched down. After the regular passengers were through customs it was our turn. The sight of thirty or so intoxicated longhairs descending on them must have been a bit daunting to the customs and passport officials. We were of course asked to remove our silly hats and we were through. We were ushered onto a coach and immediately driven to the concert. Keith Moon was in his element. He was on the coach mike and welcomed everybody; he soon had us in fits of laughter. As we wound our way through the streets of Geneva Keith was leading us through some community singing. As we pulled into the backstage area of the concert we were in full voice singing at the top of our voices the cockney version of 'Side by Side', much to the amazement of the Swiss security men.

As my band was bottom of the bill we were first on. All the bands had to use the same drum kit except The Who. (By this time Keith had a custom built massive Premier kit and apparently had stopped destroying his kits—but rumour had it, well, you could never be too sure with Mr Moon.) The vibe in The Blunstone Band at that time was fabulous. We had just finished a tour of clubs in the US where, instead of the usual one night stands, we had enjoyed the luxury of a series of one week residences. This had led to much fraternizing with the club's female staff members and the establishment of a band points club. Our bass player who shall remain nameless came first, I think I was second, then guitar and keyboards and lead singer last. As to how one scored points I shall leave to your imagination but it wasn't for having an early night in and reading the bible. In short we were enjoying life on the road but tonight was something else. We were used to small stages and we were usually close enough to have eye contact. This stage was enormous. The drums were on a huge drum riser and I had to climb up a step ladder to reach them. I remember feeling a bit unsteady on my ascent but once I was seated I peered out to the crowd. A sea of faces stretched to the horizon it seemed. My fellow band members were in position about a mile below. I instinctively tried the bass drum pedal and the sound from the fold back speakers almost blew my head off.

"Ladies and gentlemen, from England, The Colin Blunstone band." I counted out 1234 on the hi-hat and we were in. The sound was amazing; a perfect balance of bass, guitar, and keyboards. Our first song as always was 'Time of the Season' by The Zombies; of course Colin had been the lead singer. As we played the intro Colin would make his appearance and make it to his mike just in time for the first verse. However Colin had been no stranger to the bar and kind of mistimed it. It was such a long walk. He kind of half walked, then jogged, then ran when he realised how far it was. He made it, just, and the crowd loved it and probably though it part of the show. After the first song ended the crowd response was hard to judge but near the end of our 45 minute set the feedback was good and we went down well for a support band.

It was mayhem backstage with musos and road crew everywhere. Gary Glitter was next on and his band were scattered everywhere. They were easy to pick as they were all wearing outrageous silk shirts and silver trousers. The Small Faces were holding court at the bar and a number of young girls had appeared as if from nowhere mixed in with the record company executives and publicity people. This is where the action was. The green room was a large marquee tent. There was food laid out and snacks and a mini restaurant where you could chill out if you wanted. We towelled down and changed clothes. Colin was first out and joined Gary Glitter and Rod Argent in the green room. Rod had also been in the original Zombies with Colin so the three of them were like the rock establishment. The younger generation of rock stars were The Small Faces and The Who. All working class boys who went to school and grew up in council estates in the east end of London in the fifties and sixties. The Faces had hit singles including 'Itchycoo Park' and 'Lazy Sunday' but it was The Who that had reached international stardom. Pete

Townsend is a prolific writer and was the definitive angry young man. His stage presence was one of violent protest. A brilliant guitarist who had a reputation for aggression and would often repeatedly smash the guitar into the stage at full volume at the end of the show creating a wall of sound and feedback until the guitar eventually snapped into pieces. His drummer Keith would happily join in often reducing his drums to splinters by using brute force and explosives hidden into the kit. Roger Daltrey the lead singer and John Entwhistle seemed mild-mannered in comparison but were, I imagine, as hard as nails, toughened up by years on the road. The Glitter Band went on playing a long instrumental before Gary made his entrance. Gary was all showbiz, not a great singer like Colin but full of front. Unfortunately he is rather rotund but to his credit squeezed himself into a tight fitting white outfit with a large belt to cover his protruding belly not unlike a latter day Elvis Presley. The crowd reception was a bit cool and when Gary went into his big hit unfortunately called 'Do You Want To Touch Me' they waited for the chorus and on cue shouted in response: *NO!*

Most entertainers would have walked off at this rebuff but Gary just cracked up laughing and carried on with the show. In fact when the band finally left the stage the good humoured crowd applauded politely. If there was change in the air, and a revolution in music, Gary didn't know about it and certainly didn't care. The Small Faces on the other hand did and looked very dapper with their short mod haircuts and 'Pop Art' clothes. They were all slightly built as their name implies and all incredibly exactly the same size – small that is!

Argent were now pounding away on stage with Jim Rodford on bass and Bob Henrit on drums both of whom, years later, were to join Ray Davies and The Kinks. I returned to the bar and there was Colin Blunstone who was in great form. Colin's drinking would go in stages. The first three or four beers would find him at his best. Stage two you would get the famous smile except it was permanent – no matter where the conversation was going. Stage three could really lead anywhere, you got the smile, the glassy eyed look and fixed stare. At stage three Colin would happily talk all night to complete strangers and often did. However tonight he was surrounded by his peers and was definitely at stage two. I gladly joined his group of revellers. He was telling a story about George the roadie. George was the driver for The Zombies in the sixties and was their only roadie.

I had heard it before but Colin has this knack of adding small details that are extremely funny. The Zombies were in the charts and would turn up at gigs to be confronted by hordes of screaming teenyboppers. They would then try and load their gear through the crowd and set up. George it seemed only had one leg. The other was false which enabled him to drive but not lift any gear. This had gone on for some weeks and they all travelled together in a small comer van. It was summer and the boys had noticed a dreadful smell in the van that never went away. One very hot and sunny day it got so bad they had to pull over and jump out. George admitted that he hadn't had time to change his dressing and his leg stump had not been changed. His leg had gone off!!

Rod Argent had joined us just in time and confirmed it as being the most horrible smell imaginable.

Suddenly there was a roar from the crowd. The Faces had just run on stage. Little Stevie Marriot, the East End boy made good grabbed the mike as the band crashed into 'Itchycoo Park'. "What will we do there?" "We'll get high," replied 20,000 voices. "What will we touch there?" "We'll touch the sky," came the tumultuous reply. The sight from my vantage point at the side of the stage was awesome. The band was prancing about the enormous stage lit by columns of stage lights that at times swirled into the sea of excited faces. The crowd was of course loving it but there was still a feeling of excitement and expectancy in the air. This of course was for The Who. Pete Townsend, a man capable of extreme violence and breathtaking beauty in his music stood next to me for a while. Already dressed in his trademark white boiler suite and Doc Martin Boots, his face was grey, his expression drawn and pensive, etched with the lines of a life lived to the max. His worried look was replaced for a second with a smile as his old mates were falling about the stage, lost in their moments of glory. I dragged myself away from the side of the stage and met a rather inebriated Keith Moon in the toilet. He was leaning over the trough in the classic drunk pose. "They won't let me in," he slurred.

"Who won't Keith," I said. "My own bloody band. They won't let me in the dressing room." To my relief he burst out laughing. "Mind you, can't blame 'em can yer." For a brief second his deep blue eyes looked sad as if he wanted me to say no. He straightened up as if he was trying to pull himself together. A half empty bottle of brandy was sticking out of his pocket and he wobbled out where his roadies guided him to the stage.

His massive Premier drum kit was set up in the middle of the stage. I counted twelve hanging toms and six floor toms all of which were completely surrounded by banks of cymbals. In addition he had two bass drums, a kettle drum that he had to stand to reach and a massive hanging gong. The backstage bar emptied as the pre-recorded intro to 'Tommy' suddenly burst from the stage. We crowded round the side of the stage, the lights dimmed, then exploded into life as Pete Townsend ran at full-speed, guitar in hand, then went down on his knees sliding right across the stage with his guitar feeding back to the power chord intro to 'Tommy'. As if this wasn't enough suddenly there was a deafening scream from Roger Daltrey as he made his entrance. While all this was going on John 'The Ox' Entwhistle had sauntered onto stage left and plugged into to his custom built mega bass rig. All eyes now turned to the still unoccupied drum kit. Knowing how out of it Keith was, for a second I wondered if he would make it. I shouldn't have worried. The intro tape was powering out the prelude music as Keith ran from the other side of the stage and at full pelt did a somersault and almost landed upright on the drum stool. It was so close, but he held his balance, slid onto the stool and grabbed the headphones. He paused for a moment and his timing was perfect. He lashed into the drums and the band joined in—a frightening wall of sound rushed out into the night sky. The massive crowd burst into life – this is what they had been waiting for.

The chemistry between the four members of The Who has always seemed perfect to me. Like The Rolling Stones it is difficult to imagine any other line up. A perfect match. Roger Daltrey the party animal and mike swinging tough guy. John Entwistle, a man they called the Ox because of his ability to party to excess. An inventive bass player who took that instrument to new levels and still to my knowledge the only rock bass player ever to have a bass solo in a pop record (check out 'My Generation'). Pete Townsend to this day in my book is an extremely underrated guitarist who achieves in his writing the most sensitive of lyrics and songs mixed in with the violence and aggression of his upbringing and lifestyle.

And that of course brings me back to Mr Moon –and to California – and to the bar of the Whisky A-Go-Go where Clem Burk, Blondie's drummer, had been hanging on every word. He informed me that when Keith had died he had tried unsuccessfully to buy his Premier kit that I had just described but he does have a collection of memorabilia of one of the best and certainly most enigmatic drummers of all time.

California felt full of energy and open to new ideas, I had felt the same excitement in New York but Middle America was completely indifferent to us and I guess us to it. All the music press ever wanted to talk to Annie about was what the songs meant to her, or really I guess what the songs really meant. She bravely had to deal with all that pressure. We had some great new songs that we had introduced into our live gigs to see how they were received and to get them tight and well-arranged and ready to record. This had worked to an extent and we used sound checks mostly to rehearse in a new song and on the 17th of May we finally played our last date of the American tour.

Island in the Sun

We had played almost every night for two months, often with overnight trips to the next gig. The very next day our gear was flown out to Miami, Florida to be shipped out to Antigua then on down to Montserrat in the Caribbean. The island of Montserrat is a small volcanic island 11 miles long by 9 miles wide and 48 kilometres from Antigua. It was part of the British Empire from 1871 till 1958 when it became independent in name only as it was still part of the British Overseas Territories. The Beatles producer George Martin bought land and built Air Studios, a state of the art 24 track recording studio complete with swimming pool, a patio for outdoor dining, kitchens and luxury accommodation for the musicians. The population of the island was very small when we were there with only a few cars on the island. The population now is even smaller as the capital Plymouth and the airport were partly destroyed in 1989 by hurricane Hugo .As if that wasn't enough, on the 18th of July 1995 the whole island imploded in a massive volcano. This destroyed Air Studios completely and also a club house and accommodation that George Martin had built and left 20 feet of ash over the capital. Amazingly enough there were no injuries but two thirds of residents of the island left. Another eruption two years later killed 19 people and today half of the island is abandoned.

However when we arrived there in May 1980 it was idyllic. We flew from LA to Miami Airport. We were then driven across the tarmac to a small runway on which sat a twin engine Cessna Airplane. I'm sure it was the plane used for the movie *Casablanca*. We looked on nervously as our luggage was loaded. It was then that I saw a rather interesting character walking toward us. He looked perfect for one of the customers in Rick's Bar in the movie, in fact he looked as if he had just left the bar. He was wearing a very crumpled uniform of sorts. It was a light grey colour and I guess was originally white. The collar of the jacket was frayed and one of the shoulder epaulets was missing. To complete the image his pilot's hat was pushed back to one side at an angle. He treated us to a beaming smile. "Hi, my name is Jack and I'm your pilot for today's flight." I'm not sure who looked the most bizarre. We too were crumpled and a bit worse for wear and tear. Jet lagged and fazed from two months of madness. Dave, always ready with a one liner asked, "Do you think we will make it?"

I took in the pilot's rather bleary eyes and the gin stained jacket and began to wonder too. "Oh you've heard about the weather forecast, well don't you worry we will go round it." His Humphrey Bogart American accent did little to reassure us and we reluctantly climbed aboard. It was tiny inside and the seats were like deck chairs bolted to the floor. There weren't enough seats so one of us had to sit up the front next to Jack. I was last in so I had no choice. My seat belt did little to make me feel secure. He pulled out a bunch of what looked like car keys and tried the engine. It spluttered and failed to start. "Don't worry folks she's just a bit hard to start up sometimes, like my wife." I was beginning to warm to Jack; if we were all going to die we might as well enjoy it. I suggested he tried the choke. Yes – great idea.

To my amazement he pulled out a knob revealing a cable and tried again. Bingo, the engine exploded into life. The noise was deafening and the tiny cockpit rattled and shook. For some reason we all started clapping. "Thank you," he shouted over the din, "and for my next trick!" The dashboard had a small modern screen that had obviously been added since the plane had been made. It flickered into life. "There she is," he shouted.

"Is it a photo of your wife?" I asked.

"Hell no, but close. No that's the storm."

He asked me to move my bag as it was on the hand brake. Here we go. We eased forward and the radio crackled into life. Is that you Jack? Yes how are they hanging? Oh not bad. You got those limey rock stars aboard, Yeah they're here, well you tell 'em they are in for a bumpy ride. You've got a bit of weather over Plymouth with a cyclone over Puerto Rico, apart from that she's looking OK. Clear to take off. The radio went dead. I was going to suggest community singing. 'A Long Way to Tipperary' came to mind, or maybe 'Show Me the Way to Go Home'. I turned round to see how my fellow passengers were doing and immediately changed my mind.

Peet had produced a flask of brandy from somewhere and was wearing his drunken face, Dave looked cheery as if he was on a day trip to Sunderland, Annie looked

OK but was grasping Dave's hand tightly. Eddie on the other hand looked dreadful with his shoulder length virtually covering his face as if he was hiding. We taxied over to the runway and adopted the takeoff stance complete with white knuckles. Jack opened up the throttle, the noise was deafening. We shot forward and bumped our way along the tarmac at an amazing rate of knots. 'Tally Ho!' Jack shouted and pulled back the stick.

To my surprise we climbed smoothly up, up, and away and soon levelled out. The sky was blue without a cloud to be seen and the engine had quieted down somewhat. I started to relax and released my safety belt. "I wouldn't do that son if I were you." Jack pointed to the screen. On the horizon there was an ominous band of black clouds.

He got on the radio at once. Well Jack you sure enough can't climb over it, best to go around the side. Good luck, over. We banked to the left and the engines protested as we again began to climb. At this point I thought we were going to die. I have always hated heights and amusement parks. Whilst in LA our beloved record company had taken us for a day trip to the most famous of them all, Disneyworld. We all hated it. Pastel colours, plastic food, have a nice day smiles. Even meeting Marilyn Monroe hadn't done much for me, but the thing I have always been scared of are the rides. The thought of spinning or being upside down at speed has never really appealed to me. I also suffer from acrophobia. As I shut my eyes and thought of the Queen I felt a tap on my shoulder. "Jim, Jim, look." It was Dave who actually seemed to be enjoying himself. I looked out of the window and we seemed to be going sideways.

The sky was black and lightning was darting about the sky. Drops of rain were racing across my window. The tiny plane started shaking then; all at once, we were clear, the sun was shining and we levelled out again. Yes we were alive. We treated Jack to another instantaneous round of applause. He got on the mike and informed us we were going round the long way round the storm and even gave a confident sounding ETA in Montserrat.

I love Jamaican music and couldn't wait to drink in the relaxed vibes and see palm trees and sandy beaches and meet beautiful dark husky women. I had seen Bob Marley and The Wailers on their very first concert at The Hammersmith Odeon. A large contingent of skinheads in the crowd had all but ruined the night but Marley was magnificent. I had actually convinced The Tourists to try a reggae feel to one of Peet's songs called 'Ain't No Room' which can be found on our first album recorded in Germany. And here we were three years later about to record our third album coming in to land on what seemed like a desert island in the middle of the Caribbean Sea.

Jack was on the mike. "If you look to your left you will see the island of Montserrat. Discovered in 1493 by the great explorer Christopher Columbus when it was occupied by Amerindians, Columbus claimed it for Spain and called it Santa Maria De Montserrat. In 1631 you guys took control and England sent in some Irish settlers."

As in the whole of the Caribbean, African slaves it seems did most of the labour. We flew in low over the shimmering sea then over swaying palm trees whizzing through what looked like someone's back garden with some tarmac on it. Jack eased us down, we bounced a bit at first then the shaking subsided, he braked at a reasonable rate and skilfully did a 360, swinging round into the parking space in front of a wooden shed. He switched off, put the handbrake on, and announced we were now on British soil so we should feel at home!

Well, it was just like I pictured it. The wooden shed had a hand painted sign which read **'Customs'.** Two men came out and unloaded our suitcases into the customs hall. It was deserted apart from a Coke machine and a row of desks. The two men that unloaded were wearing sandals, shorts and matching Wings over America t-shirts. (We later discovered that Paul McCartney had recorded there with his band Wings.) They then lifted our bursting cases onto the desks one by one and, to our amazement, walked behind the desks and changed into what looked like army uniforms and asked us if we had anything to declare. "No," I said in my firm voice trying to make out I didn't notice the change of clothes. My suitcase was bulging with dirty washing including my still wet stage wear from the last gig. We all stared at each other and our two customs officials checked our passports and proudly stamped them. The stamp said 'Welcome to Montserrat; Member of the British Empire'. We sauntered out and sat under a tree to get out of the hot sun. Despite the humidity Peet was still wearing his regulation op shop baggy suit, I think it was the same one I had first seen him wear the first time we had met some two years earlier. The label of pop star didn't sit well with Peet. We had all gone through a lot of changes in the past two years and we had found success and a degree of fame I suppose, but there was still this creepy feeling in the band. Something just wasn't right.

Looking back now I think the band was split into three parts. Peet was a loner. He was the only one that was married and had two young boys that he had spent very little time with during the last two years. The misunderstood poet, the writer of songs. I don't think Peet ever saw himself as a musician in the normal sense. The second part of The Tourists was Eddie and I, bass and drums. We were professional musicians playing in a successful group and travelling all over the world and having fun. The third part was of course Dave and Annie. At that time we had no idea of the astronomical success that they were later to achieve both collectively and individually as songwriters. One can only assume that all this pent-up energy and talent was just below the surface and The Tourists were just scratching it. Apart from all this I was on my own mission to enjoy every moment. After all here we were, sitting under a tree on a desert island in the sun. I was half expecting Harry Belafonte to pull up and give us a lift to the studios but instead it was Tom Allom our record producer. A bus had magically appeared from the bushes with a brightly painted logo on the side, 'Air Studios Montserrat'. We clambered aboard and cruised across the island. It was truly magnificent. After two months of Holiday Inns, freeways, clubs and truck stops it seemed we were in paradise. The road was just wide enough for two cars to pass but at times only a single track with palm trees hanging low over the road. We turned off the road and down a grass driveway and there it was, like a mirage. So here it was, George Martin's dream recording studio. After all those years stuck at Abbey Road the record royalties must have just kept rolling in as he produced the most famous band ever known worldwide. We were confronted with a surprisingly modern colonial style building with the main feature being the swimming pool right next to the kitchens and the pool. Entering the studio was a trip in itself. From the heat and humidity of the Caribbean you stepped into the world of a modern recording studio that seemed like the Tardis and you were transported to what seemed like any studio in New York or London or Paris. Tom showed us round the studio which was quite large and equipped with a state of the art, 24-track recording desk. There was my trusty Premier kit all set up and miked and our backline amps and keyboards all ready to go.

Suddenly there was a shout from outside, we ran out to see Eddie being dragged out of the pool fully dressed and smiling. We asked him if he fell and he just said, "No I just wanted to get wet!" We were all, I guess, suffering from exhaustion. The guy who had pulled Eddie out of the water and maybe even saved him from drowning, introduced himself as George. He was smiling ear to ear, "I am your chef," he announced. "Is anyone else going to get wet or can I show you the accommodation?" It turned out that George was a gourmet chef and also quite an expert at mixing cocktails and was on call whenever we were in the studio. The accommodation consisted of a row of houses at the rear of the studios. We had a sort of townhouse house each and a maid each. I was in Caribbean heaven. My completely self-contained house was a stone's throw to the pool and studio; it was modern but stylish in a sort of colonial old style. I bravely loosened my bulging suitcase; the pent-up energy at once started the zipper moving until it undid itself with the pressure. An assortment of dirty shirts and magazines flew out over the bed. My stage clothes were still damp from the last gig which was two days ago and my drumming shoes were a bit worse for wear and tear and were 'definitely going a bit'. There was a gentle tap on the door, a female voice quietly asked, "Are you there?"

Her accent was beautiful and sweet and full of promise. I threw my smelly shoes under the bed and quickly tried to look presentable. I opened the door and there was my maid. 'Hello, my name is Rose.' Well Rose was not really what my imagination had conjured up. She had a beautiful and pretty face but she was rather portly and middle aged. I guess you would call Rose a Mamma. She was dressed in a multicoloured dress with a vivid red blouse and her turban was bright yellow; like George the chef she had an amazing smile. 'I've come to pick up your washing.'

We all had a very relaxing dinner sitting out by the pool in the warm evening. Eddie seemed to be back on the planet and even Peet seemed sober and together. We made a list of the songs we had 'broken in' live on the road and Peet played a few new ones to Tom the producer and John Punter the engineer who had flown out with Tom a few days earlier. That night I had the best sleep in a long time. I awoke to Rose gently tapping on my door. "Jim, it's 11 a.m., breakfast." Thrilled not to be in a Holiday Inn, I showered and there were all my clothes clean and fresh and neatly folded.

On that first day we soon got a sound and balance and by the evening I think we had at least two backing tracks down. George the chef was on call and more than a few Pina colada's had been consumed before dinner. It was a happy time for the band; we had time to relax and spend our time doing what we did best. The studio was small and intimate compared to Germany and London and had a great vibe, the only thing that was missing was we had run out of grass. Dave had asked George where we could score. He had laughed and said he would go up the mountain tomorrow. The next morning over breakfast he produced a plastic refuse bag completely full of grass freshly pulled off the mountain. There was enough for a year's supply! He proceeded to pick off the best buds and put them on silver foil and into his kitchen oven. 'Ten minutes on 2 man and away you go'.

That second day we stayed straight till after dinner recording two more backing tracks. The evening was spent smoking and smiling and laughing. We started jamming over the next few songs. It felt effortless and some new relaxed feels started to creep into the new songs. We went long into the night, eventually recording our first and only instrumental which we called 'Walls and Foundations' and the backing track for 'Angels and Demons'. Both songs were credited to Peet but the instrumental was a band composition in my book. In the cold light of day the next morning we nervously played back the two tracks. Usually when musos are that stoned the tempos suffer, usually slowing down, but they were, and still are, outstanding. Within the first week we had ten solid backing tracks down. Now came the guitar, keyboards and percussion overdubs, vocals would be last.

Smile for the Camera

News came through that a journalist from The Sunday Mail and a photographer would be coming out from London to spend a couple of days and if it went well we could get a double page spread to promote our return to the UK.

They arrived the next day. The journalist was quite a well-known writer of gossip columns for the Sunday Mail – I shall call her Julie. She had a pleasant enough way about her but there was something in her smile that betrayed her, we immediately went on the defensive. We were still smarting from the bad reviews from the English music press. The photographer was much more open and soon had us on side with some stories of unusual situations he had found himself in. I thought, oh yeah, good cop-bad cop. The next morning we had a photo shoot at 9 a.m. The plan was to pose in full stage gear in the jungle with a keyboard and some guitars. Peet looked resplendent in an immaculate black Sergeant Pepper suit and Annie went for the retro sixties look; silver sparkly top and tight leather mini skirt, black tights and high heels. The stage gear was set up in a small clearing near the studio. We had gathered by the pool and were just about to trek down to the clearing when the heavens opened. We retreated to the bar which was not a good idea. Peet decided on his usual heart starter – a double rum and coke. Eddie and I joined him and patiently waited and waited for the downpour to stop. After a few more heart starters the sun came out and off we trekked. A sudden clap of thunder and return of the rain saw us in full retreat. Julie and John the photographer now had us held captive in the bar so decided to make a day of it. Pina coladas were ordered all round. After some time again the sun returned so we decided to give it one more go. We must have looked an unlikely bunch of trekkers. Our hearts by this time were truly started and we bravely pushed on through the bush. Annie's heels were sinking in the mud and one came off and to this day must still be there under the volcanic dust. Things were not going well. John got us to pose and started shooting. Then it happened. Peet, guitar in hand started to slowly sway. It was hard to detect at first, just a gentle movement but a definite sway. I started to giggle like a schoolboy but I don't think Annie saw the funny side of it. Click-click-click we strained to look cool in the heat and humidity. Peet was by now swaying wildly. In complete slow motion he swayed forward at an amazing angle then overcompensated his return and fell backwards into the mud, as stiff as a board, still holding his guitar. Well that was it for Annie. She screamed out, 'THAT'S IT PETER,' and she spun round on her one high heel and dived into the jungle. You could have cut the air with a knife. Immediately, as if on cue, there was another tropical downpour. Julie the journalist seemed to be beaming with joy. Whether this was due to the alcohol or the possibility of a scoop was hard to tell. We picked up our muddy songwriter and staggered back to the track. I tried to picture our lovely Annie storming through the bush in her '60s outfit trying to make sense of it all, while her partners in crime sloshed their way back to the comfort of the studio.

After a change into dry clothes and some hot sobering coffee we decided on getting back to work.

Annie had returned and seemed to have calmed down. To her credit she must have finally seen the funny side of our bizarre photo shoot as the shot of Peet completely comatose lying in the mud, guitar in hand, was published in our tour magazine on our return to the UK.

We were now faced with the distinct possibility of a double page spread of drunkenness and cruelty, of us arguing with photos to prove it. I could just see the headlines:

'TOURISTS SPLIT IN TROPICAL PARADISE
STORM'

Something had to be done and quick. As I had all but finished my drumming duties on the album I was given the dubious job of PR rep and everyone pleaded with me to smooth things over.

Hat George

The next morning at breakfast I dutifully rang Julie and asked if I could take her out to lunch. She agreed and invited Annie and I to her hotel during which time she could interview us about how the band were doing and so on. I explained that Annie was worried about her voice as she had got a chill from yesterday's adventures and she would be singing lead vocals today in case her voice got worse. I persuaded her I was free and would pick her up in my mini-moke and show her the real Montserrat; I wanted to get her away from the comfort of a stuffy hotel. To my knowledge there were at that time only two hotels on the island, both in Plymouth. I had found a funky bar tucked away down a lane not far from the studio I had popped in with Eddie for a quick drink one afternoon and I remembered the laneway, the bar was called appropriately enough 'Rick's Place'.

We arrived around lunch time and decided to have an aperitif or two. Rick was the bartender and the chef and I guess the owner. He was super friendly and after our third round he suggested we try his special rum cocktail, so we did. Things were going well and after an hour or so we were still sitting on high stools at the bar. To my relief Julie seemed to have forgotten the interview and only asked the occasional question about how the band was doing. I vaguely remember enthusing about the American tour and what a success it had been and, with the help of yet another cocktail, I began to believe it myself. At this point we decided at long last to order some lunch. A few locals had arrived and the Enormous Wurlitzer jukebox was quietly purring in the corner mostly relaxed lovers rock which is a Jamaican term for laid back reggae. Then it happened. Julie leant down for her bag and screamed.

"It's gone, my bag has been stolen. My credit cards, my passport. Call the police!" At once the atmosphere disappeared. Rick asked us if an old man had dropped his hat at the bar. Julie had completely lost it and started to shout at him, "What a stupid question, now listen my good man: I am an international journalist, do you know who you are dealing with?"

At that point I remembered that a man had been behind us and had in fact found his hat and left.

I told Rick as much and his face lit up with a broad smile—"Hey lady, don't worry, it's only Hat George—I just go and get him.

"Now don't you go and upset me customers." With that he ushered us upstairs and produced a full bottle of rum, a bottle of ice cold Coke, and two glasses and left. I clearly remember announcing to Julie, "I do believe he is trying to get us drunk!"

After a while Rick returned and asked us to bring our drinks downstairs and meet George.

He was being held by a tall immaculately uniformed policeman who stood to attention as soon as we came down. Amazingly Hat George had the bag. He smiled weakly and apologised. Julie snatched it and checked the contents. Everything was there except her precious credit cards. "That's it," she screamed, "I want to press charges." She moved in on the poor old man and shouted face to face, "Where are my bloody cards?" Hat George sheepishly pointed to the corner of the bar and there were her cards neatly arranged and wedged down the side of the juke box.

I must admit my memory of the drive back to the studio is not very clear but I do remember lots of laughter as we negotiated between the fallen coconuts on the road. Julie it seemed had decided not to press charges and in the excitement we had completely forgotten to eat. I screamed my mini moke into the Air Studios driveway and tried my best to do a wheelie narrowly missing the pool. The band were having lunch on the balcony and much to their amazement Julie and I emerged from a cloud of dust and, hand in hand, stepped elegantly straight into the pool.

So that was it, I had saved the day. We got our double page spread with some great photos and no mention of any arguments or falling over. We finished the backing tracks and most of the overdubs and left our lovely island in the sun with ten songs under our belt. We were all very keen to get back to the UK having been away for nearly three months. When we landed back in Miami Airport we were immediately in trouble as our US visas had expired. We were informed that we were not allowed to leave the airport with six hours to wait for our flight. As it happened our producer Tom Allom had a girlfriend in town, he called her and we were invited over for a pick me up. I remember we stored our hand luggage and casually sauntered over to the exit then dived into two taxis. I then fulfilled a lifetime ambition and said to the driver 'follow that car', or to be perfectly honest 'follow that taxi', but it felt good. It was Miami after all. We made it and were treated to coffee and cakes and some very high quality cocaine. The six hours flew by and soon we were whizzing through Miami talking excitedly about touring England again. We were confronted by the same customs officer that had earlier seen six bleary and tired looking English people.

Now we were chirpy and awake and raring to go. Dave had bought a joke dog's lead that balanced out from his head to display a collar but of course no dog. A small crowd gathered and the ever-eccentric David A. Stewart was in his element as he was pulled this way and that by an invisible dog through the check in.

For some reason, we had decided to call our third (and final) album 'Luminous Basement' and we were keen to see how our new label RCA would promote it. Word came through that the powers that be were disappointed with the songs as there was no obvious single. We were asked to come up with a new song before the scheduled release date of mid-August 1980. A tour was also being booked of 3000 seated concert halls starting mid-September. The pressure was on. We rented Ringo Starr's studio which was built into his house in Ascot to do some final mixing of the album. It was a massive rambling place with a grand hall sort of entrance. I decided that the drums on the only instrumental track on the album, 'From The Middle Room', needed to be special so I set up my full concert kit in the hallway of Ringo's house and double tracked what I had recorded in the Caribbean. The result is a sort of early psychedelic

Eurythmics. The sound we got was amazing as the natural echo of the building was awesome. Mr Starr was not in residence at the time which was a shame of course as I would have loved to have met him. The grounds around the house were more like a park than a back garden and I found out that John and Yoko had owned the house before selling it to Ringo. We stayed over for a few nights and I had the dubious honour of sleeping in John's bedroom which had two distinctive features. One was a lone toilet bowl built into the middle of the room and the other was John's name was printed on the wall above one side of the bed and Yoko's name on the other. Downstairs the famous white grand piano that features on the video of 'Imagine' was still there and a collection of strange surrealist statues were scattered around the place. How many people do you know that have slept in John and Yoko's bedroom? Not many I guess. So there you go, I'm famous!

We desperately needed a single. At this point in time I suggested to our management company and record producer that we go out on a limb and release Annie's song 'One Step Nearer The Edge'. To me this would have been a win/win situation and to this day I think it would have been a massive hit. It would also have silenced the music press and got us away from this 'infectious fun' label. It would have also been just Annie on lead vocal which was really what CBS were crying out for. The idea was turned down flat by one and all and instead we rehearsed a quirky song that Peet had come up with called 'Don't Say I Told You So'.

Peter Coombs had done it again—a perfect made to measure 3 min 55 seconds song with a great riff or hook as we called it. The tempos of 'I Only Want to Be with You' and our follow up 'So Good To Be Back Home' were very similar and had the same straight ahead rock feel. I suggested a downbeat bass drum and ska type feel on the verses and a short 4-4 bass drum feel on the second part of each chorus. On listening back now it does seem a bit contrived and an obvious attempt to make a three minute single complete with a long fade with the title repeated over and over.

In retrospect, we had now become a parody of what we had set out to be. We had completely fallen between two stools, recording songs only aimed at the charts, which was exactly what the English music press had accused us of. We had alienated our original fanbase, which were the kids that saw us as a new movement in post-punk who listened to our lyrics and related to them in some way. We had been swept away like so many bands before us with the heady mad rush of success and somehow lost our way, or certainly our direction.

However, RCA liked the single and it was released in August 1980 but initial sales were not good. We then went on an ambitious tour with a thirty date schedule of 3000 seated concert halls some of which were half empty. Ask any entertainer how that feels. After all that work and all the heartbreak when you run on stage and are confronted with some empty seats (and some nights many empty seats) – well it's soul destroying. The single was getting good airplay and we managed to get back on Top of the Pops which got the song into the bottom of the charts from where it slowly went up a few spaces each week.

We cancelled the last two dates in Dublin and Belfast as we just weren't selling tickets.

The writing was on the wall but we refused to believe it. Arnakata immediately booked us on a long tour of Australia where 'I Only Want to Be with You' had reached no 6 in the charts; we were convinced the new single would take off.

I Wanna Go Home

I was personally thrilled to tour in Oz as my only sister had immigrated there in the '70s to be followed by my parents so it was family reunion time. They all came out to the airport and I met my two nephews aged 6 and 9 for the first time. The kids were big fans and I remember they came to the Countdown TV studios where we played live. We were interviewed by Molly Meldrum who at the time was a very important personality. If Molly liked you and the record you were promoting it almost guaranteed a hit record. We shared the show with the American band The Motels who were touring at the same time. I remember Molly sharing a joke with Martha on one side and Annie on the other. Martha camped it up and came over really relaxed whereas poor Annie was very serious and seemed very stiff in her answers, again being asked about the meaning of the songs on the album.

We hit the road and travelled all over. I found Australia to be very refreshing and totally different from the violence I had felt in the USA and totally different from old grey UK. It seemed like a young colourful country with a vibrant music scene and lots of medium sized venues and not only in the major cities. We played everywhere from Tasmania to Perth. Even though we plugged the single everywhere we played, still sales were still slow. The strain of almost three years of touring and being in each other's pocket 24/7 started to take its toll. On a flight from Sydney to Perth I noticed from my window seat that smoke was pouring from what I thought was one of the engines. At once there was an announcement that we were returning to Sydney as there was a small problem with one of the dials in the cockpit. It turned out that what I took to be smoke was fuel being jettisoned. After circling Sydney airport for what seemed like hours we made a very dodgy landing and were immediately ushered onto another plane. That flight also turned out to be eventful as just before landing we heard the news that John Lennon had been assassinated. Things came to a head one night after five consecutive gigs in different towns with travelling long distances in between. Annie ran on stage and bumped her head on the low ceiling on the stairs and collapsed.

She came good the next day but she was suffering from exhaustion, as I think we all were. Peet would disappear into the night after gigs in Sydney in search of drugs and Annie finally decided to inform us we were all drinking too much. Things were getting completely out of control and our performances started getting sloppy till one night when after a half-empty Sydney gig Peet told me he was going home. I informed him we were not in Muswell Hill but in a bar in a hotel in Australia. I went to my room and thought no more of it. At breakfast the next morning Kevin our trusty tour manager told us Peet had insisted he book him a flight and through the night had rung Arnakata. Peet really had gone home.

The Dream Is Over

We were now a four piece with a bunch of gigs still to go. At this point you might expect that the band finally found its true direction and a happy ending to the story. I do seem to remember trying to rally the troops on the way to our first ever gig as a four piece with Annie as lead vocalist. Dave easily covered for the lack of Peet's rhythm guitar but with no time for any rehearsals it was an impossible task and far too late for a change in direction. We were still playing songs written for us by an exceptional songwriter who had now abandoned us on the other side of the world. So after three years and countless hundreds of gigs we finally played our last ever gig as The Tourists in a pub in Melbourne. We made no announcements, there were no magical moments, and we just went through the setlist like robots. We were done. The dream was over.

I think we had all been secretly hoping for some sort of miracle on our return to the UK and word came through from Arnakata that we must not talk to the press apart from saying Peet was suffering from exhaustion.

I won't bore you with the details of our return. Peet had disappeared and Arnakata organized a press release which said the band had split over musical differences which wasn't far from the truth. They then hit us with a bill for thirty-eight thousand pounds which for some reason they said we still owed them. As if it wasn't enough that we had lost all our money that had been stashed in our offshore bank accounts in legal fees – they were still trying to squeeze money out of us. To say that this left a sour taste in our mouths is an understatement.

When my flight cases arrived at Heathrow my old friend Eddie the drummer from The Vibrators kindly helped me retrieve my equipment before Arnakata did. He had his band's truck with VIBRATORS written along the side. As luck would have it I had a set of white overalls not unlike the boiler suit Pete Townsend wore in The Who. It had The Tourists logo on it in big letters which was identical to the logo stencilled all over the three enormous flight cases. We just breezed in as if we owned the place and backed the truck up to the barrier gates. In the office I said the magic words "Arnakata for The Tourists". Amazingly the security officer fell for it and handed me the paperwork to sign which I gladly did. The doors slid open and we were in. We found my beautiful cases stacked up in the arrivals and we quickly put down the ramp and rolled them in. Just as we were thinking we had got away with it we were stopped in front of the exit gates and motioned back into the office.

Eddie kept the engine running and it occurred to both of us to crash our way out. Now drummers, for some reason, are not well known for their intelligence and we were sorely tempted.

I thought better of it and jumped out trying to look like a real roadie. I had forgotten to fill in the address of Arnakata's office. I panicked. I think I wrote something like Penny Lane London W1, signed the release form and ran for it.

***

With my gear safely stored I followed Peet's example and went to ground. I moved back into the house in Hendon and tried to come to terms with not playing and travelling every day. I got bored very quickly and started to hang out in nightclubs. My local club was Dingwalls Dancehall in Camden Town. The owner/manager was a wonderful man called Roger Bannister. I told him one drunken night that I had seen his famous run on TV when he became the first athlete in the world to run a mile in under four minutes. It's only recently that he owned up to me via Facebook that he was a different Roger Bannister.

There was live music at Dingwalls every night till 2 a.m. with a cover charge, however I had become such a regular customer that I always jumped the queue and got in for free. Over the years I saw The Selector, Madness, Doctor Hook, Pretenders, The Police and Elvis Costello among others. The booker for the room was Boz who was a famous agent and all round nice guy.

When Jimmy from The Pretenders died, Boz organized a pick up band to play a benefit gig there. The line-up included Larry Wallis, Wreckless Eric, some of Elvis's band the Attractions including Pete Thomas the drummer. The Pretenders' record company rang me and offered me two hundred pounds worth of cocaine as payment. I politely refused and took the cash instead. Pete Thomas from The Attractions is a great drummer

105

and it was the first time I had played along live with another drummer. There was so much Charlie going round in the dressing room I guess we all had the same offer.

One night there I was at the bar in the club when who should walk in but my fellow pirate adventurer Dave Stewart. We hadn't seen each other since I was dropped off at the airport. He asked me if I would go over to Cologne with him and Annie as they had a bunch of songs they wanted to record. I foolishly refused, telling Dave I really needed a break. I was amazed and flattered I guess, after all we had been through, that Annie would want to work with me again so quickly.

As he left I asked him if he had a name for the new band. When he told me they were thinking of calling it Eurythmics I told him it would never work as The Tourists was a simple and easy name to remember and Eurythmics wasn't. Well how wrong was I?

The Lucky Country

In **1986** I applied for immigration to Australia. The only suit I had was an old one my dad had left me when he left for Oz. It fitted quite well apart from looking hopelessly out of date. I also had my hair cut fairly short but still shoulder length so I tucked it into my collar.

One by one the bored looking interviewers came out and marched off with my fellow would-be escapees from Thatcher and her madness. I was on the point of doing a runner for the door when an attractive young woman came out. "Mr Toomey?"

I willingly followed her down the long corridors of power, trying not to notice her swaying hips.

I was praying that she was going to conduct the interview. You can imagine my relief when she entered the interview room and sat behind the desk. I began to relax. She was a stunning brunette and I was dying to ask if one of her parents was Asian. She read out the requirements that I had to fulfil to be even considered entry to Australia. She went on to explain that as all my immediate family were in Oz I had a good chance, as that gave me almost enough points for entry. For a crazy second my mind immediately went back to The Colin

107

Blunstone Band and the points system. Stop Jim! – I had to get myself together. "Now the only way you can get the additional points required," she went on, "is to have employment skills that Australia has need of." Half my hair suddenly popped out. "Now it says here that you have been a professional musician since 1965 and overnight you have become a travel agent." This was my chance. I sat back and explained what a great business idea it was to set up tours based around bands touring and how we could offer discount tickets on flights and entry to the venues in one package. I was over acting, and I think she knew it. "I see you have already spent two months in Australia with a work visa as a musician."

"Yes I was in a band at the time." I began to sink back in my chair, with half my hair out I must have looked like a demented crazy person.

"Oh, who were they?"

"A band called The Tourists," I mumbled.

"You are joking," she said, her face lit up like a Christmas tree. "I saw you at the Hammersmith Odeon." I sat up at once. "I bought your album." I loosened my tie and the other side of my hair was released. "Was that you on drums?"

"Well yes it was actually."

She asked what had happened to Annie and the others in the band and we started chatting about the lifestyle in Australia. I couldn't believe my luck, the band had finally come to my rescue in the most unexpected way. I was almost at the point of asking her out to dinner when she looked at her watch and ended the interview.

I spent the next few weeks checking the post box and finally the letter came. I had passed the interview and had permission to pick up my visa for permanent entry to Australia. As soon as I had my visa, I shipped my entire concert drum kits, all packed beautifully in the three enormous flight cases, to the port of Melbourne. This journey would take six weeks and I booked my flight.

***

I was to see Dave and Annie again when I caught up with them in Brisbane. I had heard that Eurythmics were planning a tour of Australia and rang RCA for some tickets. I got an invite to the welcome to Oz lunch organised by RCA and backstage passes for the gig at the Entertainment Centre. It was great seeing them again. Annie seemed just the same to me, almost as shy and very much under Dave's influence at that time. Dave on the other hand was totally different. He asked me how I had coped after The Tourists had split. I told him of my renewed love affair with the lovely Penny Blue and how I easily merged back into the house in Hendon with its unlimited supply of sex, drugs and rock and roll.

Then the big move to Oz and how I had been so lucky and somehow had fallen on my feet again. I had in fact met a German businesswoman and was by now living with her in Double Bay, a trendy part of Sydney. I shall call her Helga. Helga was an aerobics teacher and owner of a very successful club which at the height of the '70s 'keep fit' boom had made her extremely rich.

Dave and Annie had sold out the Entertainment Centre for the week but had Monday off. I invited them to our house for dinner, thinking they would enjoy a quiet evening in away from the hype and publicity. Dave would have none of it, he wanted to go out.

I invited him to the London Tavern as Monday night was Happy Hour. Two pints of draught Guinness for the price of one. I said, 'Dave, whatever you do come into the private bar as the public bar will be packed with musos.' At six-thirty Helga and I were nervously waiting. Underwood Street in Paddington is a narrow side street and as I peered out I saw a white six door limousine nosing its way up onto the pavement in an attempt to park. Dave was first out wearing a vivid red leather jacket with his long blond hair flowing over his shoulders. He was with a big guy that I assumed was his minder. Dave typically went straight into the public bar and had to almost fight his way to the back bar where we were. We had a few drinks and the big guy that I thought was a minder turned out to be Connie Plank, the German producer who had recorded our first album. It was one of those magic nights where everything seemed to fall into place. I introduced him to Helga and they immediately threw themselves into the German language and more drinks were ordered. The starstruck waitress came over and asked Dave if he would like to buy some raffle tickets to win a meat tray. He pulled out a wad of notes and bought twenty as I remember.

I suggested we go to have dinner at Doyle's seafood restaurant down by the harbour. I explained to Dave that it was probably the most exclusive restaurant in Sydney and was very expensive but should be available as it was a Monday. We piled into the limo and Dave played a demo of some songs he was producing. The singer sounded very familiar – it turned out to be Mick Jagger. We swanned into the restaurant and I heard the head waitress whisper to the staff – "It's Eurythmics." I started to feel famous all over again. Now I am a big fan of Australian wines and told Dave as much, but he insisted on ordering six bottles of Veuve Cliquot champagne and then asked the astounded waitress if they could make the bill very expensive, "And do you have any fish?"

Now you could be excused for thinking this a bit crass and a pop star showing off big time but this was pure Dave Stewart. He would always have an outrageous comment ready to fire off and confuse people. One night in the famous Blue Boar café on the M1 in the UK we had staggered in late at night for the usual sausage egg and chips to eat on the way home. Dave announced in a loud voice. "I want some dreadful food and I want it now! I want a thousand on a raft, a cup of rosy lee and a crocodile sandwich – and make it snappy!" The late night staff cracked up and had served him his usual baked beans on toast, and a cup of tea.

He said to me once in The Tourists, "Jim, when I am rich and famous I will build a house out of cocaine for the band to live in."

Well I'm still waiting Dave.

The End

Epilogue

Friends (and come to that complete strangers) have asked me over the years if I regret the way Dave and Annie went on to greater things and I was not included. Well my answer is no. The last time I saw Annie was in the green room at the Brisbane Entertainment Centre.

She asked me what I was up to. I explained that I am married now and a family man. I have retired in as much as I don't tour any more but I am still playing drums, mostly just weekends in small clubs with a little jazz/blues trio. Then she said the most amazing thing which I shall always remember. "Jim," she said, "I envy you, I would love to be able to just turn up in clubs and sing then go home, I am recognized now wherever I go and I have to put up with all this." She pointed to the 5000 seater concert hall.

I reminded her of what Gypsie Rose the fortune teller had said all those years ago; she smiled and said, "Yes she was right of course, Jim, I should have known!"

Next minute she was gone, spirited away to the limo.

***

I saw The Rolling Stones play in a tiny club called the Ken Colyer Jazz Club in London's Soho in 1962. Thirty or so years later I was living in Japan and they played a concert in the massive Tokyo Dome just down the road from where I was living. Now they are all incredibly well off to put it mildly, with more money than you could possibly spend in one lifetime, but even now in their seventies they are still touring sweating out all that rock n roll.

It begs the question: what is the motivation for success? Annie would love to just turn up in a club and perform without all the trappings of fame. Her and Dave are still out there, recording and touring. Even I can be found most weekends happily loading my drums into some club or bar around Brisbane. What does everyone search for in life? I have found my happiness now in Australia and family and I see my adventures in life were all connected to the journey, bringing me to this very moment in time. In a nutshell I would like to quote the Dalai Lama – "Happiness doesn't always come from a pursuit. Sometimes it comes when we least expect it."

Index